Nordic Survival

I0788898

Erudite Essays on the Origins and Survival
of a Human Kind from the Stone Age to
the Stoner Age

By

William Rapier

with an Introduction by

James LaFond

What are the origins of the most self-loathing kind of men?

Where did they come from?

When did they rise?

Where did they thrive?

Why have they ceased to strive?

Might they survive?

Renegade opinionist, William Rapier, whose publisher has turned away from the content of this investigation in stark affright, has enlisted the aid of reprobate, hobo, crackpot author James LaFond in publishing his work. For although *Nordic Survival* is a mere investigation into the trajectory of a certain segment of humanity, in William's home nation, he could be imprisoned for writing such an honestly speculative and informative book.

Copyright 2021 William Rapier

A Crackpot Book

Cover image: Botticelli's Birth of Venus

> *"When something appears white to our eyes which the church has defined as black, then this is likewise to be declared as black."*
>
> *St. Ignatius, Founder of the Jesuit Order, 1553*

Contents

On the Pink Brink

In 1453, 110 years before Ignatius developed his rules of "corpse-like obedience" to the most abstract and domesticated iteration of Christian piety, the eastern Bastion of Christendom fell. This is an odd statement to put before the child of Modernity, as the concept of Christendom went extinct beneath the seductive weight of the concept of racial whiteness between 1700 and 1900. This was easily accomplished by the merchant class of early Modernity, as Christianity had already largely reduced the ethnic identity of all Europeans with its call to the creed of the earthly universal, which was then easily distorted into the search for heaven on earth, for the realization of the utopian dream of perfection amidst plenty, of a safety achieved without distinction. Thus, by the dawn of the 21st the quest for utopia reached the high tenor of a lemming-like rush towards extinction, which is the logical result of any type of living kind that loses its distinction.

What amazes the observer, here looking back over the gaslit stern of our boat, self-perfecting distinction into the time-drowned graves of many a nation, is that as Constantinople fell, and the Turkic empires continued to expand the castration and estrangement of European men from Europe, and raped so many millions of blue-eyed and green-eyed girls that the ancient lands of Jason are now largely devoid of the fair-haired vestige of our ancestors, that hardy men from a handful of small coastal nations sailed forth to conquer or subdue the entire world, in just under 400 years accomplishing what no known body of invaders before them had accomplished in 4,000 years.

Then, these men killed each other in their suffering millions and gave the empires of their ancestors back.

Now, the scions of those bloody fools invite the descendants of those once despoiled by their grandfathers' ancestors, castrating themselves, giving over their children for rape, or declining to have children of their own.

So, willingly, even passionately, with pathos, dies a once great brotherhood of races, the conquerors of hundreds of proud warrior nations now denning flaccidly within temperature-controlled chambers of plush geometric sterility, hiding behind paper masks from the visitations of scientifically improbable murder-flights of demons, in the very name of science. So do the scions of the men whose spyglasses once sought every horizon for danger and placed their flags on every island worth naming, now simpering to a silent end between a bowl of antidepressants and a TV screen across which parade a pageant of drag queen pheasants.

So the flags come down, the skags go down and the Sons of Aryas dance the gig of the cosmic clown.

Surely, as the life cycle of nations goes, another round the Old Ones Beyond have not forgotten to frown.

May they strike full and true and cleanse the gaudiest of days with the clean smite of night.

Thank you, William, for the honor of publishing this book, James LaFond,

European Cave Art

An article in *Science* [https://www.sciencemag.org/news/2018/02/europes-first-cave-artists-were-neandertals-newly-dated-paintings-show] notes that there has been a reassessment of dates of cave paintings at La Pasiega, Maltravieso and Ardales, Spain. Using uranium and thorium dating, the paintings are now dated to 70,000 years ago. But, the mainstream politically correct ideology in archaeology holds that modern humans only entered Europe 42,000 years ago. Cro-Magnon man was not in Europe at the time, according to the mainstream, and the Neanderthals are regarded as too dumb to paint, although the article has no choice but to reject this standard view. Some think that a common ancestor of humans did the painting, but that is simply an ad hoc hypothesis. The parsimonious explanation is that the 42,000-year date is simply wrong, being ideologically motivated. Before the present PC woke madness, it was accepted that our ancestor Cro-Magnon man entered Europe around 80,000 years ago, which would explain the paintings perfectly. But, even after a few years, this refuting material is just ignored by most of our "objective" scientists.

The Metaphysics of Nordic Personhood

Individualism is a great and noble philosophy, but as seen with American libertarianism, it can go too far and just get down-right weird, when like any other doctrine it is pushed to the limits. Of course, one must be quick to add, for the five second Mission Impossible self-destruction crew, the collectivism of socialism, now rolling out across the USSA, goes too far in the other evil direction. Yet anyone with a few grains of knowledge of anthropology and human prehistory, would understand that individualism arose as a philosophy along with the emergence of capitalism. We don't see much individualism in traditional "primitive" societies, for the isolated individual, beloved of Austrian economics would not survive long. Liberal ideas would have puzzled the ancient Greeks, who undoubtable contributed some of the best examples of individualism, in acts of warrior bravery, but it was not something a whole social order was based upon.

Still, in an age where other ethnic groups identify, almost to the extent of a "hive mind," Anglo-Saxons and other Nordic/ Northern Europeans as a tribal group will disappear unless they immediately stop seeing themselves as "universal," "Americans," and other ethnically-drained descriptions. Time, in this post-traitor Trump era, to assert ethnic, not just colour, group rights and identity. Sorry, universalists from our tribe, this or destruction. But the game is now up, post-2020, and the deracination and dispossession of our tribes has got to the level of looming extinction in the Great Replacement:

https://www.theoccidentalobserver.net/2019/06/29/from-diversity-to-the-browning-of-the-white-world-the-white-replacment-and-destruction-movement-becomes-more-explicit.

As the assertion of an ethnic right to exist is foreign to conservatives, in love with money, the flag, and "muh constitution,"' for all the good this did for them with the stolen election of 2020, with the elites still laughing at them, is good to hear the cry for ethnic survival from various sources. Here is Brett Stevens on this theme, "Why the Western European Race Needs Personhood."

http://www.amerika.org/politics/why-the-western-european-race-needs-personhood/

> Let us consider first the preservation of genetic groups. Per the UN definition of genocide, any forced migration into the group destroys the group. Lawsuits could prevent that.
>
> Another might be the conservation of culture, mostly definitely an intangible folkway (behaviors, beliefs, and lifestyle joined). When our culture is replaced in schools and media by political values and propaganda, we can tell that we are being squeezed out and sue.
>
> More controversial might be using this to defend the *spirit* of a place, or the combined expression of race, customs, religion, ethnicity, and beliefs as fit into a "blood and soil" view of the area. Germany must always *be* Germany which

requires it be German in genetics, actions, and thoughts.

As the years of Leftist revolution and dominance wind down, people are looking for a new direction and a transition plan (as is usual when there is change). Perhaps the two can be combined by expanding our legal systems to include the facets of life that Leftism has for so long denied.

This seems to be a great insight that we should slowly digest, but not too slowly, or our tribe might disappear down the sewer of history, completely.

Lessons from Ötzi the Iceman
about Ancient Germanics

While the contemporary anti-Germanic genocide regime portrays ancient Germanics, like present day Germanics, as savages, only fit for migrant replacement, the facts of the most ancient European mummy, Ötzi the iceman show otherwise. The remains were found frozen in a glacier on the Alps on the border between Austria and Italy, the Ötz Valley, and dated to be about 5,000 years old.

Scientists have been able to work out much about life at the time by an examination of his remains. For example, his intestinal contents contained red deer, chamois meat, and einkorn wheat bran, which he most likely ate as bread. There were also hop-hornbeam pollen grains in the stomach contents as well.

These grains had an intact intracellular content, so that they were eaten while still fresh. So, the iceman died in the spring at the time of the hop-hornbeam harvest. The einkorn wheat was harvested during late summer, so this must have been stored for almost a year. Thus, his society practiced agriculture at a time where mainstream archaeology says Germanics were only hunters and gatherers. Further, the clothes of the iceman were sophisticated for the time, for anywhere in the world, with the coat, belt, leggings and shoes made of various types of leather. The shoes were so advanced that a Czech academic who reproduced a pair, stated that they were probably made by a professional shoe-maker. A Czech company wanted to purchase the rights to manufacture these types of shoes.

There is debate about whether or not the iceman's axe was bronze or copper. The copper age in Europe is said by mainstream archaeology to have begun about 1,000 years after the iceman's death, and since bronze is made by smelting tin and copper together, having a bronze axe turns archaeology on its head, and so long as the results are pro-European, that is always resisted by modern racially suicidal Euro-academics. Ancient Egypt had bronze around 3150 BC, and Mesopotamia, 2900 BC, so the Germanic iceman was well ahead of these so-called "cradles of civilisation."

Thus, Ötzi came from an advanced society for the time, relative to anywhere else in the world, one which was not "savage." We descendants of the Germanics need to have a bit of racial/tribal pride, or the future will be that there will not be even any fossil remains of our kind. Interestingly enough, the iceman was killed by being shot in the back with an arrow, and that is significant too, in our present age of treason.

Ancient Egyptians were White!

I have been reporting on lesser-known archaeological research which serves to re-moralise Northern Europeans, who have been deracinated and dispossessed by the ruling globalist elites. Thus, I have countered those who have argued that Northern Europe was a backwater. But, taking the fight to the critics is the book by Arthur kemp, *The Children of Ra: Artistic, Historical, and Genetic Evidence for Ancient White Egypt*:

https://www.amazon.com.au/Children-Ra-Artistic-Historical-Evidence/dp/1644404060

What is particularly good about this book is that it reviewed genetic evidence for ancient Egyptians being primarily white. It has been known for some time that several surviving Egyptian mummies, including the pharaoh, Rameses II, had golden or red hair. While it is trendy to claim that race is only a modem concept, the evidence points against this, as extensively documented in A. A. Sayce and R. Peterson, *Race in Ancient Egypt and the Old Testament*, (Scott-Townsend Publishers, 1993).

New evidence for the Kemp thesis continues to pile up, with scientists finding European DNA in Egyptian mummies, according to the paper by V. J. Schuenemann (et al.), "Ancient Egyptian Mummy Genomes Suggest an Increase of Sub-Saharan African Ancestry on Post-Roman Periods," *Nature Communications*, May 30, 2017, Article 15694. The title would seem to support the mainstream view, in the early period, ancient Egyptians were more closely related to Europeans than Africans, but there was an influx of sub-Saharan genes after the Roman period, long after Egypt's period of greatness.

A Swiss study of the pharaoh Tutankhamen shows him to be related to 70 percent of modern British men, 50 percent of other western European men, but only one percent of contemporary Egyptians, so that King Tutankhamen and modern British people have a common ancestor.

http://www.reuters.com/article/2011/08/01/us-britain-tutankhamun-dna-

The research, which was conducted by the iGENEA Centre in Zurich, Switzerland, reported that Tutankhamen's distinct genetic marker haplogroup R1b1a2, was thought to have originated in the Caucasus or north of the Black Sea, which are regions also believed to be the origins of the Indo-European peoples.

The Genetic Origin of the British

In an article by Nicholas Wade, "A United Kingdom? Maybe," *The New York Times*, March 6. 2007, at:

https://www.nytimes.com/2007/03/06/science/06b rits.html

Wade says that geneticist have reached a view that the standard view of British history is wrong; that Britain and Ireland are descended from different people, "the Irish from the Celts and the English from the Anglo-Saxons who invaded from northern Europe and drove the Celts to the country's western and northern fringes."

Wade gives the alternative view advocated by Stephen Oppenheimer of the University of Oxford, "the principal ancestors of today's British and Irish populations arrived from Spain about 16,000 years ago speaking a language related to Basque." Allegedly, there was only minor, insignificant genetic additions from the Celts, Romans, Angles, Saxons, Jutes, Vikings and Normans. Also quoted in the Wade article is the view of Bryan Sykes, also of Oxford University, who says: "[t]he Saxons, Vikings and Normans had a minor effect, and much less than some of the medieval historical texts wold indicate." Sykes is author of *The Seven Daughters of Eve*, and *Adam's Curse*, the later which predicts a generic "end of men." The Y chromosome is supposed to be disintegrating. Well, there goes the human race! I remain unconvinced, as much as feminists may get excited by this thesis.

However, Sykes has also published, *Saxons, Vikings and Celts: The Genetic roots of Britain and Ireland,* (Norton, New York, 2006), based on a DNA study conducted by Sykes and his Oxford University team and 10,000 volunteers across the United Kingdom. There he tells us that "Genetic dates are not very accurate." (p. 155) Nevertheless, the genetic analysis goes somewhat against the position of the Wade article. First, the Celts (and this term is vague and ill-defined, he admits), are not related to the Celts who spread to Italy, Greece and Turkey. "The peoples of the Isles who now feel themselves to be Celts have far deeper roots in the Isles than that ... their ancestors have been here for several thousand years." (p. 281) There were a large proportion of Irish Celts who came from Iberia who did join the Mesolithic people who were already there. But, talk of a connection to "Spain" (p. 282) is nonsense. Spain did not exist then, and the whites of Iberia are not the same as the Spanish of today. So, the British people are not Spanish or Mediterranean.

Sykes' book points out that 10 percent of the men in the south of England are patrilineal descendants of the Saxons and Danes (genetically too close to distinguish), increasing to 15 percent in the north, 20 percent in east Anglia and in the Viking settlements, reaching 42 percent in Shetland and 37 percent in Orkney. (p. 194) Hence, the Saxon and Dane invaders did leave a substantial genetic presence (p. 286), contrary to Wade. And Sykes also states: "England owes very little to Celtic, but almost everything to its Germanic roots." (p. 260)

However, the work of both Oppenheimer and Sykes has been taken to show that most of Britain's ancient population arose from the earlier Iberian ice-age migrations in Palaeolithic times.

Nevertheless, as argued in Mark Thomas (et al.), "Evidence for an Apartheid-Like Social Structure in Early Anglo-Saxon England," *Proceedings of the Royal Society Series B*, vol. 273, 2006, pp. 2651-2657, Anglo-Saxons, Jutes and Friesians probably replaced around 50 percent of the male lines within a century after the Romans left Britain. The indigenous Britons were at a disadvantage compared to the Anglo-Saxons, and consequently began to be bred out of existence. Genetic evidence is based on the Y chromosomes of English men being identical to those of Norway and Friesland, where the Anglo-Saxons came from.

Michael Weale (et al.), "Y Chromosome Evidence for Anglo-Saxon Mass Migration," *Mol. Biol. Evol.*, vol. 19, no. 7, 2002, pp. 1008-1021, found that Y chromosome haplotypes were "statistically indistinguishable" between central England and the Frisian samples, but a dissimilarity was found between central England and North Wales: "Using novel population genetics models that incorporate both mass migration and continuous gene flow, we conclude that these striking patterns are best explained by a substantial migration of Anglo-Saxon Y chromosomes into central England (contributing 50%-100% to the gene pool at that time) but not into North Wales. (p. 1008)

However, both Thomas (et al.) and Weale (et al.) assumed that "the Germanic import into Britain was only significant during the early Anglo-Saxon period, and that no significant intermarriage occurred between the British and Germanic peoples": J. G. Pattison, "Is it

Necessary to Assume an Apartheid-Like Social Structure in Early Anglo-Saxon England?" *Proceedings of the Royal Society Series B*, vol. 275, 2008, pp. 2423-2429. Pattison's estimation of the native Briton population is two million and the migrating populations, between ten and low hundreds of thousands, which he says is in agreement with Thomas (et al.). But as I read them, the Anglo-Saxon Germanic input is much larger, and if periods other than the early Anglo-Saxon period are added, logically must be greater.

Thus, there appears to be no consensus among geneticists about these issues. One thing is clear though: genetics does not trump other historical and cultural evidence. As I see it, contrary to Wade, the common-sense historical view still stands. But I wonder how long it will be before it is proposed that the original inhabitants of Briton were actually sub-Saharan Africans? Maybe it has already been done.

Chimps Must be Human Too,
by the Lewontin Argument!

Richards Lewontin famously argued that there is more genetic variation between individuals, than between races, so, races don't exist. He did not say that explicitly but that is where the Left took the argument.

https://pubmed.ncbi.nlm.nih.gov/12879450/

https://en.wikipedia.org/wiki/Human_Genetic_Div ersity:_Lewontin%27s_Fallacy

Let us run with Lewontin's argument. Why restrict it to the human race? Isn't that speciest, a form a "racism?" Sure. There is a very close relationship between the genomes of the genera *Homo* (humans) and *Pan* (chimps), having the high genetic similarity as noted by D. E. Wildman (et al.), "Implications of Natural Selection in Shaping 99.4 % Nonsynonymous DNA Identity between Humans and Chimpanzees: Enlarging Genus *Homo*," *Proceedings of the National Academy of Sciences*, vol. 100, 2003, pp. 7181-7188:

> What do functionally important DNA sites, those scrutinized and shaped by natural selection, tell us about the place of humans in evolution? Here we compare 90 kb of coding DNA nucleotide sequence from 97 human genes to their sequenced chimpanzee counterparts and to available sequenced gorilla, orangutan, and Old World monkey counterparts, and, on a more limited basis, to mouse. The nonsynonymous changes (functionally important), like

synonymous changes (functionally much less important), show chimpanzees and humans to be most closely related, sharing 99.4% identity at nonsynonymous sites and 98.4% at synonymous sites. On a time scale, the coding DNA divergencies separate the human– chimpanzee clade from the gorilla clade at between 6 and 7 million years ago and place the most recent common ancestor of humans and chimpanzees at between 5 and 6 million years ago. The evolutionary rate of coding DNA in the catarrhine clade (Old World monkey and ape, including human) is much slower than in the lineage to mouse. Among the genes examined, 30 show evidence of positive selection during descent of catarrhines. Nonsynonymous substitutions by themselves, in this subset of positively selected genes, group humans and chimpanzees closest to each other and have chimpanzees diverge about as much from the common human–chimpanzee ancestor as humans do. This functional DNA evidence supports two previously offered taxonomic proposals: family Hominidae should include all extant apes; and genus Homo should include three extant species and two subgenera, Homo (Homo) sapiens (humankind), Homo (Pan) troglodytes (common chimpanzee), and Homo (Pan) paniscus (bonobo chimpanzee).

Apart from the genetics, there are similarities between human and chimp brain structure, internal organs, and other aspects of physiology. Thus, many scientists are now proposing that *Pan troglodytes* and *Pan paniscus* be moved to the genus *Homo*, or even that Homo sapiens be transferred to *Pan*.

https://www.sciencedaily.com/releases/2003/05/03 0521092615.htm#:~:text=2-,DNA%20Demands%20Chim ps%20Be%20Grouped%20In,Genus%2C%20Say%20Wayn e%20State%20Researchers&text=Summary%3A&text=G

Proposed changes in the primate order are stirring up evolutionary debate. Humans and chimpanzees should be grouped in the same genus, Homo, according to WSU researchers in a May 19 article (#2172) published in the Proceedings of the National Academy of Sciences. Although WSU's Morris Goodman, PhD, has already proven with non-coding DNA sequences that chimpanzees are closest in kinship to humans rather than to gorillas, evolutionary traditionalists say chimps and humans are functionally markedly different and therefore belong on different branches of the family tree.

New analyses show humans and chimpanzees to be 99.4 percent identical in the functionally-important DNA, which codes for proteins and is shaped by natural selection. This provides further evidence for revisions in our genus classification. Dr. Goodman proposes that all living apes should occupy the family Hominidae (which currently contains only humans), and that both humans and chimpanzees should occupy the genus Homo.

In traditional taxonomic schemes that are still widely employed, humans are classified as Hominids, while orangutans, gorillas, and chimpanzees are classified as Pongids. Genetically, however, chimpanzees are more closely related to humans than they are to gorillas. "The accumulating DNA evidence provides an objective non-anthropocentric view of the place of humans in evolution. We humans appear as only slightly remodeled chimpanzee-like apes," Dr. Goodman said.

The WSU research team compared 97 functional genes in six different species: humans, chimpanzees, gorillas, orangutans, old world monkeys, and mice.

Based on genetic mutation tracking rates, the scientists constructed an evolutionary tree that measured the degree of relatedness among the six species. Chimpanzees and humans were the most closely sharing 99.4 percent identity at nonsynonymous (functionally important) sites and 98.4 percent at synonymous sites (functionally much less important).

Researchers determined that humans and chimpanzees diverged from a common ancestor roughly five to six million years ago, which in turn diverged from gorillas about six to seven million years ago.

"Revisions to our classification system would have far-reaching implications, much more important, in fact, than proving that humans and chimps are barely divergent. Such revisions would ensure that objective, scientific measures of similarity and dissimilarity are used, rather than anthropocentric, subjective observations. Sound genetic analysis should always be the basis for understanding the place of humans in evolution," Dr. Goodman asserts.

These taxonomic changes had been proposed previously by several evolutionary experts, including Dr. Goodman, but a difference of scientific philosophies is at play. Traditional anthropologists argue that chimps are functionally different than humans because, for example, they lack spoken language and their genetic disease susceptibilities are different.

In contrast, Dr. Goodman opens his article with a quote from Charles Darwin that says: "As we have no record of the lines of descent, the lines can be discovered only by observing the degrees of resemblance between the beings which are to be classed. For this object numerous points of resemblance are of much more importance than the amount of similarity or dissimilarity in a few points."

Dr. Goodman is a distinguished professor in the Wayne State University School of Medicine's Department of Anatomy and Cell Biology and the Center for Molecular Medicine and Genetics.

In 1962, he sparked great debate when he originally asserted that chimpanzees and gorillas are genetically more closely related to humans than to other apes. His research has since been widely accepted and his work in this area has not only impacted the study of humankind's place in nature, but also has important implications for medical science.

Thus, naturally enough, the rejection of the existence of human races leads to a further form of anti-racism, where by the Lewontin argument, we will fast be accepting the universalism of all species, like the Deep Greens propose. In fact, philosophers such as Peter Singer have extended the anti-racist argument into a more general one for animal rights. In reply, in articles at this site, I have noted that plants exhibit some of the properties that give animals rights, having a prototypical form of mentation. So, we are led to biological universalism. But, one can always turn round the conclusion and maintain that all this is absurd, that humans and chimps do fundamentally differ, having more differences than similarities, regardless of genetics. And that genetics is mainstream genetics too, not the alternative morphogenetic field theory as proposed by Rupert Sheldrake in *A New Science of Life* (1981), where humans and chimps would clearly have vastly different morphogenetic fields.

On that basis we should reject Lewontin's anti-race argument.

Are Atheists Genetic Mutants?
Will Mutants Destroy Civilization?

Atheists in their war against Christians, like to portray Christians as low in intelligence, believing absurdities, according to materialist science, and alleged superstitions. But an alternative take has been given to this by the "Jolly Heretic" Dr Edward Dutton, in his paper, "The Mutant Says in His Heart - There is No God."

https://link.springer.com/article/10.1007/s40806-017-0133-5

The idea here is that atheism is the product of a high mutant load, that is that the atheist's genome has mutated. Dutton's methodology was to examine people with high mutational loads, such as auto-immune disorders, poor immune systems and genetically-based disease, and to examine any alleged correlation with holding atheism.

Industrialisation leads to relaxed selection and thus the accumulation of fitness-damaging genetic mutations. We argue that religion is a selected trait that would be highly sensitive to mutational load. We further argue that a specific form of religiousness was selected for in complex societies up until industrialisation based around the collective worship of moral gods. With the relaxation of selection, we predict the degeneration of this form of religion and diverse deviations from it. These deviations, however, would correlate with the same indicators because they would all be underpinned by mutational load. We test this hypothesis using two very different deviations: atheism and paranormal belief. We examine associations between these deviations and four indicators of mutational load: (1) poor general health, (2) autism, (3) fluctuating asymmetry, and (4) left-handedness. A systematic literature review combined with primary research on handedness demonstrates that atheism and/or paranormal belief is associated with all of these indicators of high mutational load.

Overall, this hypothesis poses a nasty problem for the sustainability of civilisation, as observed by Dr Michael Woodley of Men, that mutational build-ups erode civilisation. Nicholas R. Jeelvy (https://www.counter-currents.com/2019/03biospenglerianism/) points out that under Malthusian conditions of natural selection, healthy men are created, and healthy men build industrial societies. But, these societies then allow the proliferation of mutants, and this ultimately leads to the collapse of such societies. This is the fundamental paradox of civilisation, and had not yet been solved. Humanity seems to go through the endless cycles of creation and then destruction, never being able to halt the inevitable decline. And, we are on the downward slope now, with very little concern about it from those who could act. In fact, the intelligentsia are doing all they can to pull civilisation down as fast as possible, as we will now see in Biden/Harris America.

African Eve Loses Her Mitochondria Fig Leaf!

Standing behind the African Eve hypothesis — the globalist mainstream view that humans evolved in Africa, which then became the mother continent — is the idea that there is only maternal inheritance of mitochondrial DNA. This is DNA in the mitochondria, not the chromosomes. The received position is that mitochondrial in human sperm, in the tail, gets excluded, a view held even in leading genetics journals.

But, it is not correct, as shown in the paper by F. Ankel-Simons and J. M. Cummins, "Misconceptions about Mitochondrial and mammalian Fertilization: Implications for Theories of human Evolution," *Proceedings of the National Academy of the Sciences*, vol. 93, 1996, pp. 13859-13863. They state: "The "missing mitochondria" story seems to have survive — and proliferated — unchallenged in a time of contention, between hypotheses of human origins, because it supports the "African Eve" model of recent radiation of *Homo sapiens* out of Africa." (p. 13859)

An example of a mainstream biologist accepting the female-only mitochondria myth is Richard Dawkins, *The Blind Watchmaker*, (Norton, New York, 1986, p. 176, where he writes that the sperm is too small to contain mitochondria, so mitochondria is on the female line, and can be used to trace ancestry down female lines, as done with the African Eve hypothesis. But this assumption is empirically false, as Ankel-Simons and Cummins conclude: "All theories of the timing of human evolution that depend on the premise that the sperm midpiece does not contribute to the embryo must be re-evaluated or rejected." (p. 13862) However, as far as I can ascertain, this critique has been ignored by the African Eve camp, being an inconvenient piece of counter-evidence, that disturbed their woke, politically correct biology.

In any case, there may be recombination or swapping of sperm and egg mitochondrial DNA, which also destroys the African Eve hypothesis. The hypothesis is at complete variance with an unbiased examination of the fossil record, which shows wide hominid migrations. Catastrophic events could have eliminated the other humans leaving the predominant "Eve" line, falsely showing that humans evolved from this line, rather than it being merely a residue

Nordics in Ancient China

I have been presenting evidence of the ancient Nordics, or Indo-Europeans as the founders of a number of civilisations, such as India. There is evidence of a Nordic impact upon China as well. First, the Nordic/Indo-European presence.

David Comas (et al.), "Trading Genes Along the Silk Road: mtDNA Sequences and the Origin of Central Asian Populations," *American Journal of Human Genetics*, vol. 63, 1998, pp. 1824-1838, analysed mtDNA in samples of Kazakh, Vighurs, lowland Kirghiz and highland Kirghiz: "Central Asian mtDNA sequences present features intermediate between European and East Asian sequences, in several parameters – such as the frequencies of certain nucleotides, the levels of nucleotide diversity, mean pairwise differences, and genetic differences." (p. 1824)

Comas (et al.) stated that the most plausible hypothesis to account for this is "extensive levels of admixture between Europeans and East Asians in central Asia, possibly enhanced during the Silk Road trade and clearly after Eastern and Western Eurasian human groups had diverged." (p.1824)

Contact thus accounts for the fact that "nucleotide polymorphism in mtDNA sequences in central Asian population is intermediate between those reported for Europe and those reported for Eastern Asia." (p. 1818)

Beyond mtDNA evidence is dental evidence, as outlined in C. Lee and E. R. Scott, "Brief Communication: Two-Rooted Lower Canines – A European Trait and Sensitive Indicator of Admixture Across Eurasia," *American Journal of Physical Anthropology*, vol. 146, 2011, pp. 481-485. Two-rooted lower canines are much more common in Europeans than other races, and thus can be used as an indicator to evaluate gene flow between Europeans and other groups. Samples from Europe are found with an average frequency of 10 percent; in sub-Saharan African populations, the characteristic is unknown and in Asian and Asian-derived populations, the frequency varies from 0.0 to 1.0 percent.

Lee and Scott found that the average frequencies of two-rooted canines along the western frontiers of China and Mongolia ranges from 0 - 4 percent. "These data suggest European-derived populations migrated into western China (Xinjiang Province) and Mongolia (Bayan Olgii Aimag) sometime during the late Bronze Age (1000 - 400 BCE)." (p. 481)

Lee and Scott conclude: "Archaeological excavations support the large-scale movement of people into this area during the Bronze Age (ca 2200 BCE - 400 BCE). Burial artefacts and settlement patterns suggest cultural and technological ties to the Afanasievo culture in Siberia, which in turn is linked archaeologically, linguistically, and genetically with the Indo-European Tocharian populations that appear to have migrated to the Tarim Basin ca 4,000 years ago." (p. 483)

A number of blonde and red-haired mummies, with straight Nordic noses were found in the Tarim basin of western china, dressed in clothes indicating high social status. This is documented in a number of books, such as Elizabeth Wayland Barber, *The Mummies of Urumchi: Did Europeans Migrate to China 4,000 Years Ago?* (Macmillan, London, 1999). The possibility exists, according to some archaeologists, that Europeans could have introduced to China technologies such as the wheel, as the migration of Europeans to China may have begun when wheeled wagons were first used, about 5,000 years ago.

Terrien de Lacouperie, *Western Origins of the Early Chinese Civilisation from 2,000 BC to 200 AD*, (Asher, London, 1894), believed that his comprehensive study showed: "The comparatively late beginnings of the Chinese civilisation showed themselves to be the outcome of an importation, not a distinctive growth from common seeds, but simply a loan, a derivation, an extension eastward from a much older form of culture in the West." (p. 1) Further evidence of an European influence on the development of Chinese civilisation is given in William Montgomery McGovern, *The Early empires of Central Asia* (University of North Carolina Press, Chapel Hill, 1939), which quotes from Turkish and Chinese records on the role of whites in ancient China.

This material directly challenges the thesis accepted by many white nationalists, of the intellectual superiority of East Asians.

Sunday Book Club

In preparation for the end of the world, or more likely, the end of my world, I am cleaning up my books, and finding a home for them. Some will wind up sent to Uncle Len, who will use them for burning in his shed, in an old 44 gallon oil drum. For warmth and light in winter, and maybe to keep the mossies at bay in summer. Some, I imagine, he will tear up, and put on the dirty cement floor, to keep his tootsies toasty in winter. I am pleased that great literature always finds a natural home.

So, what first to briefly note and throw out? Here is my copy of Alain de Benoist, *Beyond Human Rights*, (Arktos, London, 2011). De Benoist is a leading French New Right theorist, who likes being photographed with his cat. Me, I hate cats, being highly allergic to their fur which always seems to get everywhere, just like human rights.

Human rights are taken by the elite today to be natural, timeless rights. However, the intellectual elite also adopt the idea of multiculturalism, that human (with the exception of Nordics/Northern Europeans) are ethno-cultural beings who gain their identity from their culture. This, though, introduces cultural relativity, and a contradiction with the universalism of human rights. Hence, paradoxes such as "slavery as practiced in ancient Rome and Athens has become the very symbol of degeneration, and yet purchasing a child conceived in the womb of a woman who is renting her uterus is held to be a right in some modern Western countries." (p. 15)

Islamic views of man, do not sit well with modern liberal conceptions either, and sharia law conflicts with standard Western jurisprudence. As well, the ruling relativism of the age conflicts with the universalism of human rights: "subjectivity leads necessarily to relativism (everything is valid), reaching in this way the egalitarian conclusion of universalism (all are important). Relativism cannot be surmounted except by the arbitration of one's self or of our selves: my point of view should prevail for the sole reason that it is mine (or that it is ours). The notions of justice and the common good are destroyed in one blow." (pp.21-22)

The human rights of the human rights lobby are arbitrary, and are primarily devised to aid globalisation: "In history 'rights' have too often been that which the masters of the dominant ideology had decided to define in this way. Associated with the expansion of markets, the discussion of human rights constitutes the ideological armour of globalisation. It is above all an instrument of domination, and should be regarded as such.' (p. 24)

My next book is by Troy Southgate (ed), *The Radical Tradition: Philosophy, Metapolitics and the Conservative Revolution*, (Primordial Traditions, 2011). Why did I buy this book, and not try and read it before my brain began its rapid decline? Also, there are probably better people to read and review this than me, like Chris Knight. Anyway, struggling on, this book is a kind of Alt Right treatise covering topics and philosophers dear to their hearts, like Spengler, Heidegger, Ortega y Gasset, Schopenhauer, Nietzsche and so on. Here is the opening paragraph by Gwendolyn Toynton, for those who think that some of us are pessimistic, and/or over the top:

> Our civilisation is dying. I make no atonement and pull no punches for this dramatic and bold opening assertion. Our day is gone, the empire has fallen – may its death knell awaken the survivors from their slumber. Amongst the ruins of an empire toppled, a world in tatters awaits our rebirth, ready to herald in a new aeon. But we wait in vain. No savior comes forth to answer our desperate calls. We lie dreaming in the gutter and extend our reach towards the stars, which shine eternal and watch our children suffer under the eyes of the gods – all the time waiting for a change, a sign which never comes. The blind and deaf cannot hear the portents of the winds, and we are dying, waiting by the roadside because we refuse to rise. We worship impotence and utter our prayers to failure under the veil of obscurity. Thus do we fade away in silence, our protest and dreams still born in the womb of apathy. (p. 7)

What is missing from the text and most contributions is that they are preoccupied with the decline of the West, without seeing that things have got infinitely worse since Oswald Spengler (1880-1936) wrote *The Decline of the* We face now a total threat against civilisation itself, with danger on every front: race, economics, ecology, biology, with no stone of crisis remaining unturned. No amount of smart philosophical footwork escapes this problem. I did not find a real recognition of the depth of the problem, which is revealed each day in new horror articles released at sites such as NaturalNews.com. Perhaps none of this survives, and all that is left after the great crash is small tribal groups? That would preserve traditionalism then, wouldn't it? Too much abstract philosophy and not enough concrete economics, ecology and street wisdom, is a recipe for the disaster depicted in the paragraph quoted above by Toynton.

Next, I read Troy Southgate's *Tradition and Revolution: Collected Writings* (Arktos, 2010). By this time of the day I had eye strain, a head ache caused by neck pain, and had probably drunk too much alcohol to do justice in a review, but when have I ever let that stop me? This book is complex as well with many history essays dealing with nationalist themes. There is also fiction and poetry, which is good. But my attention went to the last section "activism," to see what answers this guy had on the blood and soil issue.

First, there will need to be personal sacrifice, even giving up one's life for higher ideals. Then there will need to be programs of decentralisation to break up the globalist power nexus. A return to community and small is beautiful. Real sustainable living. The globalist system will inevitably come toppling down like the towers in *The Return of the King*: "it will always be the case that chaos inadvertently contains the redeeming elements of sanity and redemption, and this unifying spirit will engender a common identity and enable people to pull together and fight back (p. 227)." I sure hope so.

This rebooted my mood and energy, and so I looked at Jonathan Bowden, *Western Civilization Bites Back*, (Counter-currents, 2014). Oh no, more philosophy, Nietzsche. A quick pit stop for a tin of cheap Asian sardines – I could feel the mercury and heavy metals giving me renewed strength – and with a glass of cheap plonk, I am off again.

The Bowden book is a collection of his essays and speeches on various Alt Right topics, such as cultural

Marxism. I simply did not find anything spectacular to report about at this late stage of a long day. Maybe sardines from Asia are not good for one's thinking? Reading this book I wondered if anybody will publish my collected essays, or will they, like me be forgotten the next day?

Michael O'Meara, *Toward the White Republic*, (Counter-Currents, 2010), has a nice cover, with three Roman soldiers reaching out to take swords from some guy who looks like he is from the Roman senate. Symbolic stuff, no doubt. The opening this time got my attention: "these essays speak to the impending demise of European America. ...Common to all of these essays is the author's intent to make whites more conscious of their destiny as a people – and to remind them, thus, of what needs doing to ensure the continuation of their kind, unique gift of Europe's blood and spirit."

The author advocates forming an ethnostate for whites, once the poorly managed enterprise known as the United States collapses in a centrifugal dispersion of its decaying and perverted powers. (p. 2) It is simply easier to break away from the old decaying countries than to fight for them back in the present culture, given the present levels of degeneracy and lack of manhood. Further, it seems an inevitable bit of history too.

The presented essays weave in and out of this theme, and I tried to work out how O'Meara believed history would play out. I did not find much beyond the idea that some type of social cataclysm may awake the masses. (p. 98) That is unlikely for most would just die without leadership. As he says: "In this pre-collapse interlude, before the fall, nothing can be done to halt the inevitable or mitigate the immitigable. We are facing, in America's world decline, not a solvable problem, but an unavoidable predicament that promises to rip apart the illusions that have animated American life for at least the last two generations – especially the illusion that unlimited growth and limitless consumption are possible in a world of finite resources." (p. 138)

That, of course, is where things will really get interesting, but all of the nationalist types do not think beyond that point. It is the new form of thought censorship – never contemplate the endgame in the richness of its full horror.

On Melanesian Blonde Hair

This article goes back to a little snip that I was sent from an Aussie friend, from *The Australian*, way back on May 5, 2012, p. 69, about blonde-hair found among the dark-skinned people of the Solomon Islands. I returned to find the article, which I put aside, when one of my students from the Solomon Islands, a really nice lad, said that there were a lot of people with dark skin and blonde hair. He said that while some of them claimed to have European ancestors, he dismissed this and put the blondness down to diet. It seems that most of the lighter haired people often acted in a superior way, which deeply annoyed my student. More probing revealed that his girlfriend had gone off with one of these blonde types and he did not like them.

Researching this I found the scientific article, E. Kenny (et al.), "Melanesian Blond Hair is Caused by an Amino Acid change in TYRpl," Science, vol. 336, p. 554. It seems, to cut the complexities, that the blonde hair is the product of a genetic mutation in gene TYRP1, and that's that. But since then, I have run into a biologist from the Solomon's, visiting here in Canada, who had blonde hair and dark skin, and said that as a child he sang songs about his European ancestors. Even though he was a biologist, who knew much more science than me, he reacted aggressively to the mutation claim, and said that this line of thought was undermining his heritage. Now there is a pretty pickle for you!

Who says that the exploration of racial differences is not fascinating, revealing the complexity and genuine diversity of the human species, with all the politics thrown in for good measure.

Anglo Saxon Speech Genocide

Here is another one attacking the past of Anglo-Saxons to serve the ideological function of deracinating them, by simply eliminating the term that once described them. This comes from an Irish academic, Mary Rambaran-Olm, who was raised in here in Canada.

https://www.dailymail.co.uk/news/article-7663127/Academic-says-Anglo-Saxon-dropped-links-white-supremacy.html

The term Anglo-Saxon is 'bound up with white supremacy' and should be replaced with 'early English', academics have argued.

Anglo-Saxon traditionally refers to groups from Germany, Denmark and the Netherlands who settled in Britain at the end of Roman rule.

However, early medieval England specialist Mary Rambaran-Olm, an independent scholar and author, claimed the term is used by white supremacists to refer to white British people and should be banned.

The academic – raised in Canada and now based in Ireland – says previous objections to the term Dark Ages sets a precedent.

She told The Times: 'Generally, white supremacists use the term to make some sort of connection to their heritage (which is inaccurate) or to make associations with 'whiteness' but they also habitually misuse it to try and connect themselves to a warrior past.'

Miss Rambaran-Olm said people in early England – or 'Englelond' – did not call themselves Anglo-Saxons but tended to refer to themselves as 'Englisc' or 'Anglecynn.'

The academic said the term became more popular in the 18th and 19th century and was used to link white people to their 'supposed origins'.

Hitler wrote of the 'Anglo-Saxon determination' to hold India, while imperialist Cecil Rhodes also regularly used the term.

John Overholt, curator of early books and manuscripts at Harvard's Houghton Library, backed a ban on the term.

'The term Anglo-Saxon is inextricably bound up with pseudohistorical accounts of white supremacy, and gives aid and comfort to contemporary white supremacists,' he wrote on Twitter. 'Scholars of medieval history must abandon it.'

Earlier this year the International Society of Anglo Saxonists took a poll of its 600 members, and 60 per cent of the group agreed to remove the reference to 'Anglo-Saxon' from its name.

But Tom Holland, author of books including Athelstan: The Making of England, said the term was 'inextricably bound up with the claim by Alfred ... to rule as a shared Anglian-Saxon identity'.

'Scholars must be free to use it,' he said.

In a tweet, he wrote of the idea to ditch the term Anglo-Saxon: 'Mad as a bag of ferrets, as they say in Deira [a former kingdom].'

I am glad that there are some scholars resisting this nonsense. The mere fact that white supremacists, a term not defined by these multicult researchers, but could mean anything, including those who wish to have a

White identity, just like Blacks, refer to a term does nothing to debunk it. These people also use so should that be rejected too? Sure, some multicultists see even that as racist. And, in an age where there is the social construction of genders, giving a near infinite variety, supposed by the woke science establishment, it is not consistent to deny those who which to categorise themselves as Anglo-Saxon, and is in fact discriminatory by their own standards.

Leaving politically correct BS academia to one side, there are adequate scientific reasons, in the old school sense of science, to use the term "Anglo-Saxon," with a recent genetic study indicating that Anglo-Saxons make up about 40 percent of English DNA:

http://www.occidentaldissent.com/2020/01/19/the-genetic-history-of-the-united-kingdom/comment-page-1/

> What does this big recent genetic study tell us about the nations of Britain? The whole island was originally populated by Britons before the arrival of the Romans.
>
> The Anglo-Saxon impact on Britain makes up about 10 to 40 percent of English DNA. The Viking impact on the Orkney Islands was about 25 percent of Orcadian DNA and was much more limited elsewhere. The Romans appear to have had no genetic impact on Britain.
>
> Does that mean the English, Scots and Welsh are mostly Britons of Celtic ancestry? It doesn't appear that way. It looks like the Celts who migrated from the continent may have had a smaller impact on Britain than the Anglo-Saxons. The vast bulk of our ancestry comes from the Bell Beaker culture that expanded into Britain from Central Europe around 4,500 to 4,000

years ago and exterminated the Neolithic people who previously lived there.

The English and Danes had only diverged about 400 years before the Viking Age which makes it difficult to tell them apart. Similarly, the Britons and Anglo-Saxons had only diverged around 2,000 years before from the same group that populated Northwestern Europe.

This headline sums it up, and why the woke politically correct may be disturbed by the Anglo-Saxon tribe maintaining any degree of self-identity.

https://www.telegraph.co.uk/science/2016/03/14/britons-still-live-in-anglo-saxon-tribal-kingdoms-oxford-univers/

Britons are still living in the same 'tribes' that they did in the 7th Century, Oxford University has found after an astonishing study into our genetic make-up.

Archaeologists and geneticists were amazed to find that genetically similar individuals inhabit the same areas they did following the Anglo-Saxon invasion, following the fall of the Roman Empire.

In fact, a map showing tribes of Britain in 600AD is almost identical to a new chart showing genetic variability throughout the UK, suggesting that local communities have stayed put for the past 1415 years.

Many people in Britain claim to feel a strong sense of regional identity and scientists say they the new study proves that the link to birthplace is DNA deep. ...

Geneticist Professor Sir Walter Bodmer of Oxford University said: "What it shows is the extraordinary stability of the British population. Britain hasn't changed much since 600AD.

"When we plotted the genetics on a map we got this fantastic parallel between areas and genetic similarity.

And the research has finally answered the question of whether the Romans, Vikings and Anglo-Saxons interbred with the Britons or wiped out communities.

The team found that people in central and southern England have a significant DNA contribution from the Anglo-Saxons showing that the invaders intermarried with, rather than replaced, the existing population.

https://www.independent.co.uk/news/uk/home-news/new-genetic-map-britain-shows-successive-waves-immigration-going-back-10-000-years-10117361.html

"The results are astonishing. They show how Britons in different parts of the country have evolved in relative isolation, for a combination of geographical, cultural, and linguistic reasons, over huge periods of time. We may think of the modern era as one of unrivalled mobility, but for much of our history Britons have proved champions at staying put.

One distinct genetic group can only be seen in what is now West Yorkshire. This is deeply puzzling. But the historians and archaeologists in our project eventually worked out that after the decline of the Roman Empire there was a Celtic Kingdom, called Elmet, exactly in this region. It seems the genetic patterns we see today have been shaped by the geopolitical landscape of millennia gone by.

Another Celtic Kingdom, Rheged, matched a genetic group in modern Cumbria. There were also separate Celtic Kingdoms at that time in North and South Wales (Gwynedd and Dyfed), where we found different genetic groups.

As for the Kingdom of Dalriada, which flourished in 550AD in what is now Northern Ireland and Western

Scotland, we found a contemporary genetic group matching that, too.

Thus, the Oxford University research showed, migrants aside, that White British are still living in the same "tribes" they were in 600 AD:

https://theday.co.uk/stories/britons-are-still-angles-saxons-and-celts

English people are mainly of Germanic origin:

https://www.theguardian.com/commentisfree/2015/mar/22/britain-tribal-millennia-anglo-saxon

Thus, those who want to abolish use of the term "Anglo-Saxon" are really advocating the elimination of a people. Resist it!

The Good Old Days:
Racialism in Philosophy

Like the rest of academic studies, philosophy has long ago been taken over by liberal globalist cosmopolitanism. But, it was not always so, and some of the greats of the past were racial realists.

https://www.amren.com/news/2020/10/philosophys-systemic-racism/

https://aeon.co/essays/racism-is-baked-into-the-structure-of-dialectical-philosophy

It is by now well known that some of the greatest modern philosophers held racist views. John Locke (1632-

1704), David Hume (1711-76), Immanuel Kant (1724-1804), G W F Hegel (1770-1831) and many others believed that Black and Indigenous peoples the world over were savage, inferior and in need of correction by European enlightenment. No serious philosopher today defends these explicitly racist views but, with good reason, they continue to study the writings of these authors. In order to hold on to the philosophical insights, scholars tend to make a distinction between the individual racism and the philosophical systems. Hegel might have been wrong for his racist writings about Africans and others, but that doesn't tell us anything about his speculative metaphysics.

Or so the argument goes. But if we have learned anything about racism over the past few decades, it is that a focus on individual racist statements can obscure the ways in which racism continues to persist in systems. While laws in the United States, for example, may no longer overtly disenfranchise people of colour, they still enable oppression through mass incarceration. Is there any risk that something like this has happened in philosophy – that in focusing on condemning the individual racism of philosophers we have allowed systemic philosophical racism to remain intact?

Let's consider in some detail the case of Hegel, arguably the creator of the most systematic philosophy in modern thought. Hegel certainly was an explicit racist. He believed, for example, that Black Africans were a 'race of children that remain immersed in a state of naiveté'. He further wrote that Indigenous peoples lived in 'a condition of savagery and unfreedom'. And in The Philosophy of Right (1821), he argued that there is a 'right of heroes' to colonise these people in order to bring them into a progress of European enlightenment.

It is not immediately obvious, however, that these racist remarks leave any trace on Hegel's philosophical system. In his encyclopaedic writings on metaphysics, aesthetics, history, politics and even botany and magnetism, he worked to show how there existed a universal process of dialectical transformation. Hegel's dialectics are notoriously complicated, but we can roughly define them as the bringing together of opposites in order to show how the contradictions between things eventually break down, and lead to the creation of a truer and more encompassing idea. One frequently cited example is what is sometimes called the 'master-slave dialectic', a discussion of the path to equal relations between two people that Hegel included in various writings. In these passages, Hegel shows how the opposition between master and slave fosters unbearable and unstable conditions that must eventually break down, lead to rebellion and, hopefully, create a system of equals.

From this example, one might reasonably conclude that Hegel's philosophical system couldn't have been racist. The critical theorist Susan Buck-Morss has gone so far as to argue that Hegel was writing the Haitian Revolution into his philosophy through the master-slave dialectic. Even if he held racist views, Hegel's philosophical pursuit of truth led him to argue for universal justice through revolutionary struggle. If this is the case, then his philosophical system might reasonably be seen to contradict his racism. It is precisely because of such dissonance that commentators justify the distinction between Hegel's explicit racism and the meaning of his philosophical system.

This distinction breaks down, however, if we look more deeply into where Hegel's idea of dialectics originated. In so doing, we will find that colonial racism directly informs the very concept of dialectics. Just like systemic racism in the world today, understanding the systemic racism of philosophy cannot be done by simply looking at a single individual or set of beliefs. We have to understand the historical context of ideas, how racism informed their genesis, and how that racism continues to structure our thinking today in ways that we might not fully realise.

I lost interest in the article after that point, but it does not matter. It is hard to believe that racism is somehow built into Western philosophy, and if it is, then so what? Turn the burden of proof towards the critic. Yeah, prove it. Then prove your proof, and so on. Infinite regression, circularity or begging the question, so gotcha! That's philosophy for you. If they cannot justify induction, then how can they refute White racism or Black racism? If there are no objective values, then how do they critique racism? The whole house of cards collapses in upon itself. Philosophers need to stop pretending that their discipline contributes anything positive, as it is mainly a negative discipline establishing what we do not and cannot know.

Philosophy is bull shit, as this post proves: https://webhome.phy.duke.edu/~rgb/Philosophy/axio ms/axioms/Philosophy_is_Bullshit.html

Slaves of the "Native" Americans

When one thinks of slavery in North America, of course the narrative is dominated by the Black slave trade, although there were more White slaves than Blacks over the course of American history, they were just called indentured labour or something like that. The Irish were treated particularly bad, as an article at your site has recently documented:

https://blog.alor.org/index.php/the-irish-slave-trade-by-patrick-doyle

We should be aware that the native Americans engaged in slavery long before Whites came to America, so that they were the first slave traders in America.

https://www.naturalnews.com/2020-10-12-native-americans-kept-slaves-people-of-color.html

"In fact, some Native American tribes were holding war captives as slaves even before European colonization. They were often used to carry out labor; some were also tortured in religious rites. After Europeans began to settle the continent, some Native Americans were captured and sold by their fellow Native Americans into slavery to Europeans.

Moreover, some tribes held African American slaves. Historical records show that Native American groups like the Seminoles, Cherokee, Creek and Chickasaw made great efforts to assimilate into white society and this included adopting their enslavement of Africans as well. It was at this point that the Native American slavery practices started to become more like the European ones and distinguish slaves more often based on race.

This created a lot of tension, particularly in the south, as different Native American tribes viewed the ideology behind African enslavement differently. While some Native American nations would give sanctuary to runaway slaves in the 1800s, others would capture them and bring them back to their white masters; some would simply re-enslave them for their own benefit. Others, however, incorporated them into their societies.

"The Five Civilized Tribes were deeply committed to slavery, established their own racialized black codes, immediately reestablished slavery when they arrived in Indian territory, rebuilt their nations with slave labor, crushed slave rebellions, and enthusiastically sided with the Confederacy in the Civil War," museum curator Paul Chaat Smith said. Some ... even practiced cannibalism."

https://www.smithsonianmag.com/smithsonian-institution/how-native-american-slaveholders-complicate-trail-tears-narrative-180968339/

You can be sure, that while Christopher Columbus is slammed in schools and universities, these institutions long ago infested with Cultural Marxism, as being a "racist," nothing will be said of native American slave owners, let alone Black slave owners owning other blacks. It refutes the politically correct narrative.

The Ancestor Effect

Going through my files I came across a remarkable paper that I intended to discuss years ago, but postponed it until it was forgotten, until now. Perhaps I should think of my ancestors more. I now explain.

The paper in question is by P. Fischer (et al.), "The Ancestor Effect: Thinking about Our Genetic Origin Enhances Intellectual Performance," *European Journal of Social Psychology*, vol. 41, 2011, pp. 11-16. The hypothesis is a remarkable one for a mainstream journal: thinking about one's genetic origin, ancestors, increases intellectual performance by providing a "positive psychological resource." This is the reason why people search for information about their ancestors and while most of us have photographs of our ancestors, used to navigate our identity. Our ancestors typically lived through tough times and exhibited resilience and resourcefulness. And "because we are the success of our ancestors and thus their genetic heritage, we tend to attribute successful problem-solving of our ancestors to our problem-solving abilities." (p. 12)

The psychologists set out to test the ancestor hypothesis, whether thinking about our ancestors increases test subjects' expected as well as actual intellectual performance. We are not interested in the actual experimental methodology employed because we are impatient to know the results, without the headache of the statistical methodology to cloud things. Basically, their studies involved tests with people thinking about their ancestors, with the control test being "thinking about your last visit to a supermarket." (p. 12)

The conclusion of the study was that "thinking about our genetic origin can have substantial psychological effects on intellectual performance, promotion orientation and the experience of control." (p. 150) The psychologists concluded that people facing situations requiring high level performance could use the technique of thinking about one's ancestors, even those one did not know in the distance past, to increase intellectual performance.

I take this as one more piece of evidence, that race, a generalisation of genetic heritage, is real and has causal effects.

How Everything Can Collapse

A number of writers at this site are collapsologists, seeing Western civilisation in deep trouble from numerous factors, such as centralisation of power, insane elites, ethno-racial replacement, you name it. The feeling is that all other civilisations in the past have collapsed so why should ours be any different?

Just in case this is thought by some to be an eccentric fringe view, collapsology is now a legitimate mainstream field, as detailed in this book by Pablo Servigne and Raphael Stevens, *How Everything Can Collapse*, (Polity Press, London, 2020). This is a mainstream book, which I do not have, but from what I read, deals with areas where we are in dispute, such as climate change. But this does show the larger issue that the issue of collapse is a live one, when both Left sand Right converge to the same point, although they come from very different perspectives, obviously enough.

https://www.theguardian.com/world/2020/oct/11/humans-werent-always-here-we-could-disappear-meet-the-collapsologists

The belief that we are heading for some kind of all-consuming crisis is not exclusively French, of course. Serious scientists all over the world are discussing it. Wealthy Americans were buying spots in Armageddon-proof bunkers long before Covid-19, and militant environmental and social protest movements have been on the rise everywhere. Within Europe, however, a survey published last November by the left-leaning

French think-tank the Jean Jaurès Foundation found that only Italy beat France for pessimism about the future. Seventy-one per cent of Italians and 65% of French people agreed with the statement that "civilisation as we know it will collapse in the years to come"; 56% of Brits shared that apocalyptic vision – slightly ahead of Americans, at 52% – while Germans came in last with a sanguine 39%.

In 2015, two Frenchmen, Pablo Servigne and Raphaël Stevens, who describe themselves as independent researchers, co-wrote an essay entitled How Everything Can Collapse, in which they introduced the term "collapsology". In a long interview Servigne gave to *Philosophie* magazine this year, he explained that, at first, their neologism was tongue-in-cheek. The concept must have struck a chord, though, because within a couple of years he found himself at the head of a movement, and this summer the word *collapsologie* entered the popular French dictionary Le Petit Robert. "We created a monster," Servigne told Philosophie.

For the authors of the Jean Jaurès study, the political scientist Jérôme Fourquet and the pollster Jean-Philippe Dubrulle, collapsology is driven at least in part by economic factors. The least apocalyptically minded country they polled, Germany, also has (or had, pre-Covid-19) the strongest economy, while the countries where the movement has the largest following – Italy and France – are those where economic performance has been poorest of late, and social and political tensions run high.

They deliberately left their statement vague as to the causes of the coming collapse, because people in different countries think differently about these. In Britain and Germany, the emphasis is on the climate crisis, as seen in the emergence of Extinction Rebellion in the UK. But in France, where they overlap to some extent with the gilets jaunes movement, collapsologists also consider society to be sick. The idea is that rampant consumerism, ever-accelerating technological advances and the dominance of neoliberalism are leading French people to perdition.

It is probably for this reason, say Fourquet and Dubrulle, that France stands apart from the other countries they surveyed in one important way: whereas in general the movement is strongest in the under-35 age group, "in our country, all generations, the 65-and-overs included, share the same sombre diagnosis".

The movement also cuts across political boundaries, embracing everyone from the far right to the far left. One of the most outspoken collapsologists is Yves Cochet, a politician with Europe Ecology – France's green party – and a former environment minister in Lionel Jospin's left-wing government of the early 00s. He has retreated to a farmhouse in Britanny and reputedly has not seen the inside of a plane since 2009. But there are also French "survivalists" who – at least until about a decade ago – shared the drawbridge mentality of the Americans stocking up on peanut butter and ammo.

After the financial crisis of 2008, says Bertrand Vidal, a sociologist at the University of Montpellier who studies these groups, the predominantly right-wing, libertarian survivalists shifted closer to Servigne and Stevens's softer, back-to-nature school of how-to-avert-the-worst, with its emphasis on sustainability. Differences between them remain, but one thing they share is a neo-Malthusian conviction that there are too many people on Earth. Even those who overtly criticise capitalism believe in a post-apocalyptic winnowing of the human species, in which nature will determine who lives and who dies. "They use the analogy of the grasshopper and the ant," Vidal says, referring to the fable in which the ant survives the winter because it prepared for cold weather, while the improvident grasshopper expires."

https://www.resilience.org/stories/2020-08-10/how-everything-can-collapse-excerpt/

Despite the high quality of some of the philosophical reflections on this topic, the debate on collapse (or 'the end of *a* world') fails because of the absence of factual arguments. It is stuck in imaginary or philosophical speculation without any real factual grounding. The books dealing with collapse are usually too specialized, restricted by their point of view or discipline (archaeology, economics, ecology, etc.), while more systematic discussions are full of gaps. Jared Diamond's bestseller *Collapse*, for example, sticks to the archaeology, ecology and biogeography of ancient civilizations and does not address some of the essential questions of the current situation. As for other popular books, they usually tackle the question by adopting a survivalist position (telling you how to make bows and arrows, or how to find drinking water in a world plagued by fire and the sword), giving the reader all the thrills of watching a zombie movie.

Not only do we lack any real inventory – or better, any systematic analysis – of the planet's economic and biophysical situation, but above all we lack an overview of what a collapse might look like, how it might be triggered and what it would imply in psychological, sociological and political terms *for the present generations.* We lack any real applied, transdisciplinary science of collapse.

We here propose, by drawing on information from many scattered works published across the world, to create the basics of what, with a certain self-deprecating irony, we have called 'collapsology' (from the Latin *collapsus,* 'a fallen mass'). The goal is not to indulge in the mere scientific pleasure of accumulating knowledge but rather to shed light on what is happening and might happen to us, in other words, to give meaning to events. It is also and above all a way of treating the subject as seriously as possible so that we can calmly discuss the policies that need to be implemented.

The issues that emerge whenever the word 'collapse' is so much as mentioned are many and varied. What do we know about the overall state of our Earth? Or the state of our civilization? Is a collapse in stock market prices comparable to a collapse in biodiversity? Can the conjunction and perpetuation of 'crises' actually drag our civilization into an inescapable whirlpool? How far can all this go? How long will it last? Will we manage to maintain our democratic reflexes? Can we live more or less peacefully through a 'civilized' collapse? Will the outcome inevitably be entirely negative?

The issue of collapsology has been discussed by writers at this site for at least ten years, before most of the above writers, and it was always a concern of a generation of critics, who saw the forces of centralisation, what we call the nasty package of globalism today, as a force eroding the moral foundations of civilisation, as surely as white ants eat away the foundations of a wood framed house. And, now is the moment of truth, as we face it, with most people, even so-called thinkers, pretty much numb to the issues.

https://www.zerohedge.com/markets/everything-we-assume-permanent-actually-fragile

Is Red Hair Now a Disease?

I have had this Nordic racial article to do for some time now, but with all the excitement of the coming collapse of the West, China war, the rise of communist totalitarianism, medical fascism, and probably other things which slip my disc, I did not get to it until now. Disclaimer; I have red hair, well, now mainly grey, but I am a defender of gingers until the end.

The claim I am going after is that red hair may have a genetic connection to melanoma and Parkinson's disease. Well, just imagine if the claim was made about African American hair, or even the black hair of the Chinese. Whoooooa! But, red heads, they won't bite back. Think again, buddy.

Even the normally medical sceptical NaturalNews.com carried this story, back in February 22, 2019, to my disappointment: "Red Hair Gene May have Connection to Melanoma and Parkinson's Disease":

https:///naturalnews.com/2019-02-22-red-hair-may-have-connection-to-melanoma-and-parkinsons-disease.html.

The research I want to attack was published as:

Xiqun Chen (et al.), "The Melanoma-Linked "Redhead" Influences Dopaminergic Neuron Survival," *Annals of Neurology*, (2017): DOI: 10.1002/ana.24852.

For starters, the genetic research involves not human subjects, but mice, cooked up to carry the alleged "red hair" gene variant of the melanocortin receptor MC1R. Apparently this gene reproduced the production of the neurotransmitter dopamine in the substantia nigra. This is an area where Parkinson's disease destroys the dopamine-producing neurons. To make matters worse, variants of the MC1R gene are supposed to determine skin pigmentation, with the red-hair variant producing a pigment known as pheomelanin, which allegedly provides less skin protection, and may have a link to melanoma development. As red-haired people usually have the lightest skin colour of the Nordic Whites, melanoma is a potential problem, even without some alleged genetic link, but, even if there were a genetic link, there usually needs to be an environmental causal agent, such as UV light exposure, and paradoxically, many red-haired people eschew the insane cult of sun baking and cover up, so that this so-called weakness can become a strength. It would be the crudest of genetic reductionist arguments to see this as in any way a problem for red haired people with double digit IQ, which is the vast majority of us. Next.

https://www.elitedaily.com/life/culture/redheads-stronger-more-successful-than-everyone/957407

https://pulptastic.com/blondes-aint-dumb/

So, what do we make of the claim that the MC1R gene in the mice had a propensity to lower the production of dopamine in the substantia nigra of the mice in the experiment? Well, mice studies are suggestive, but not definitive, and no valid inference can be made for the sorts of claims, misstating the research, that red hair causes Parkinson's disease.

For a start, this is known to be absolutely false, since people of all races get the disease, including Blacks and Asians, with no red hair at all, so that the disease is worldwide. And it is not red heads who have the highest incidence of Parkinson's disease, but Hispanics:

https://www.ncbi.nlm.nih.gov/pmc/articles/PMC28 65395/#:~:text=Using%20a%20large%20insurance%20dat abase,1.1%20and%202.3%20%5B9%5D.

According to Kumar and Clark, *Clinical Medicine* (sixth edition, 2005), the cause, if there is one cause of his disease is not known, there "are few real clues to the cause of idiopathic Parkinson's disease." (p. 128) Some genetic factors that may be relevant, not excusive to red heads, are mutations of the alpha-synuclein gene and UCHL1 gene, and other genes such as GBA, LRRK2, PRKN, and SNCA. MC1R is but one of many.

https://link.springer.com/article/10.1007/s00441-004-0917-3

Environmental factors, perhaps interacting with the genetic, may also be causative, so causation may be multifactorial:

https://link.springer.com/chapter/10.1007/978-3-211-45295-0_23

The best that could be made of this material as a genetic hypothesis about red headed people is that they have a greater propensity to Parkinson's disease because of the MC1R gene. Many studies have failed to find a link between the MC1R gene and Parkinson's disease, and even if there was a link established, the risk is likely to be small relative to a whole host of other genes.

Finally, is the cause of red hair in humans the sole result of one gene, MC1R, when most complex phenotypical traits are caused by multiple gene interactions? "Red hair color is not an example of a simple genetic trait. While the amount of red pigment may be mainly determined by one gene (MC1R), there are a large number of different MC1R alleles, and other genes affecting the amount of brown pigment that plays a major role in determining hair color. The complicated genetics means that it is possible for two red-haired parents to have non-red-haired children."

https://udel.edu/~mcdonald/mythredhair.html

That is yet another problem with the research supposedly linking red hair and Parkinson's disease, as it adopts a simplistic causation of red hair.

https://blog.helix.com/epistasis-hair-color/

https://www.nature.com/articles/s41467-018-07691-z

https://www.iflscience.com/health-and-medicine/the-genetics-of-being-ginger-are-more-complicated-than-we-thought/

Apart from all of this, there are numerous health benefits from having natural red hair, including greater pain resistance than most other hair colored people, and incredibly, being able to produce their own vitamin D, which will come in handy in nuclear winter after the global nuclear holocaust.

https://www.telegraph.co.uk/health-fitness/body/the-surprising-health-benefits-of-being-ginger/

https://www.gq.com.au/grooming/hair/science-confirms-redheads-are-equipped-with-some-weird-genetic-superpowers/news-story/cbc60110544260d0b5eb06f7f0e79845

https://www.zmescience.com/science/redheads-feel-more-pain-20092017/

The Lewontin Fallacy in Medicine

The politically correct woke nonsense to be discussed here, is pre-Covid-19, dating back to 2019, which as we will see is somewhat ironic, given emerging evidence of a racial link to Covid-19 susceptibility. Anyway, a major US medical conference heard biologists and anthropologists proclaim that that race is not a legitimate medical category, since, in short, races do not exist as discrete entities (what does?), and even so must be social constructions because, well, White racism, racial prejudice and all that jazz, as general health warnings, such as to African Americans over heart disease, may fuel racial prejudice, and one thing leads to another in an infinite chain of racist causation, with cops shooting people for trying to murder them with a knife, and members of the tribe burning and looting cities, as seen in Philadelphia late October 2020. It happens because, "orange man bad."

https://www.dailymail.co.uk/article-6710147/Scientists-say-race-does-not-determine-health-doctors-say-fueling-racial-prejudice.html

Others less drunk on social construction BS follow the Lewontin argument, made by Marxist evolutionary biologist Richard Lewontin in 1972, that based upon a study of blood groups of people from seven racial Lewontin allegedly found 85 percent of genetic variation in the difference within groups, and 15 percent between groups. He concluded, totally fallaciously, that there was no "genetic or taxonomic significance" between races. But, for starter, the only inference that could be made on the basis of the data, was in relation to blood groups, not other traits. And even here the argument is circular, since there were seven races initially chosen, and if races do not exist, who is to say what individuals were considered in the study, for in principle they could all be so genetically different as to not fall into a "racial" category. It is paradoxical to presuppose the concept of race, to then show that it does not exist.

https://onlinelibrary.wiley.com/doi/epdf/10.1002/bies.10315

Secondly, even if for many traits there was greater differences between individuals that between racial groups, that would not show that races did not exist. A variation of 15 percent is not insignificant. After all, we are constantly told by the geneticists going to the next level and raving about the unity of life, that chimpanzees and human share 99 percent of their DNA, but the phenotypical and behavioural differences are profound. It is where the differences lie that counts.

Bear in mind that race is not the only biological category to be attacked by the cultural Marxist, only the first. Now we have sex and gender being deconstructed, with some arguing for multiple gender categories, and some going further rejecting the division between men and women because intersex individuals exist. That is like arguing that colours do not exist because they are vague and there are intermediate colours. It is not just racial categories that are vague because almost everything else on the planet is vague as well, including material objects. So material objects don't exist? Some philosophers, eager for publications argue this, another BS.

The cultural Marxist view contrasts with a more moderate view that holds that there are average genetic differences between races on certain traits. While environmental factors such as racial stereotyping may hypothetically cause some diseases, we suppose, perhaps influencing hypertension, there are clear examples, such as lactose intolerance in Asians. One would have thought that knowing risk factors or ethno-racial groups, would have been a valuable aid in dealing with disease and ill-health, even if it was only an approximation. However, everything is so woke and race crazy now, that any health defect is seen as "racism." So be it: let doctors stop the "racist" practice of warning say African Americans to be aware of the risk of hypertension, Asians for cardiovascular disease, and Hispanics for diabetes. Better to get the disease than be "racist."

https://vdare.com/articles/the-bangladeshi-neanderthal-connection-yet-more-evidence-of-a-genetic-factor-in-covid-19

A startling new study casts further light on the race differences in Covid-19 incidence. Discussion of these race differences was repressed by our Race-Denying Ruling Class until it became clear that some minorities were disproportionately impacted, at which point it was proclaimed to be the fault of whites. But it remained possible that these differences were the result of deep-seated cultural practices. Now it increasingly appears they are at least in part genetic. Which means the one-size-fits-all public policy response was wrong.

England has a large "South Asian" population—recent ancestors from India, Pakistan, and

Bangladeshi—about 8% of the population on the 2011 census of England and now likely considerably higher. These people are 20% more likely than whites to die of Covid-19 and 12 years younger than whites when admitted to hospital with it [*South Asian people in UK 20 per cent more likely to die of coronavirus, study finds*, by Sarah Knapton, *Telegraph,* June 19, 2020].

This disparity is definitely not due to poverty. South Asian doctors and nurses working for Britain's National Health Service are also far more likely to die of Covid-19 than are white medical workers: they are 21% of NHS workers but 63% of COVID-19 deaths among NHS workers.

Intriguingly, British citizens of Bangladeshi extraction have been particularly hard hit. Age-adjusted, they are 4 times more likely to die of COVID-19 than whites, whereas for Indians the risk is merely 1.6 times more.

Needless to say, the Leftist British newspaper *The Guardian* claimed that the high Bangladeshi-heritage death-rate was because Corona "is a disease that thrives on pre-existing inequalities within society."

However, the new study reveals something very different: 63% of Bangladeshis—the highest of any group studied by far—carry a series of genetic variants which lead to serious risk of respiratory failure when infected with Covid-19.

And they've inherited these from the Neanderthals.

The study—The major genetic risk factor for severe COVID-19 is inherited from Neanderthals [September 30, 2020]—has recently been published in the important journal Nature. Researched by Hugo Zeberg of the Karolinska Institute in Sweden and fellow-Swede Svante Pääbo (right) of Germany's Max Planck Institute, the study draws upon earlier findings whereby a cluster of genes on Chromosome-3 have been found, if you have specific forms of these genes, to be a serious risk for respiratory failure if you contract Covid-19. This was proven using a sample of 3,199 hospitalized Covid-19 patients and controls.

The new study builds on this by establishing precisely which segments of this gene cluster confer the risk, where they have come from, and to what extent there are population differences in their prevalence.

The results are yet another nail in the coffin for those who argue that "race" is mainly a "social construct" (except when white people pretend to be non-white, when it mysteriously is wholly biological) and that any biological race differences are trivial. One such race-denier is Britain's half-South Asian science writer Dr. Adam Rutherford—who himself became seriously ill with COVID-19.

The Swedish researchers found that the relevant genes on Chromosome 3 are all strongly associated with each other, because they all entered human populations via "gene flow"—that is, intermixing—from Neanderthals. Accordingly, they constitute a "haplotype"—a group of genes that come together.

The at-risk genes are strongest in the kind of Neanderthal that lived around Croatia, in Southeast Europe, about 50,000 years ago. This Neanderthal—known as the *Vindaja 33.19*—carried 11 of the 13 polymorphisms (forms of a gene) that are associated with severe Covid-19 symptoms.

Only three of these polymorphisms were found in the *Altai* and related Neanderthals, who derive from around Altai mountains in Siberia.

The team then analyzed 5008 haplotypes in the Human Genome Project to see which human groups were most likely to carry the Covid-19-risk haplotype that appears to have been inherited from the *Vindaja 33-19* Neanderthal.

No Sub-Saharan Africans carry this haplotype, consistent with evidence that there has been very little gene flow between Sub-Saharan Africans and Neanderthals.

However, this haplotype was found at a rate of 4% among Native Americans, 8% among Europeans—50% among South Asians.

Among Bangladeshis it was particularly high: 63% of Bangladeshis carry the Neanderthal haplotype that is associated with serious complications from Covid-19 and 13% of them are "homozygous" carriers of it.

This means that they have inherited it from both of their parents. A gene is composed of two alleles, with one allele being inherited from each parent. These Bangladeshis have two copies of each of the same risky set of alleles, implying that they will experience particularly pronounced problems with Covid-19.

Part of the reason for this is surely that, in Britain's Bangladeshi community for example, a remarkable 60% of mothers are married to their first cousins, meaning that the children are much more likely to inherit two copies of any mutant, or otherwise problematic, allele which either parent might carry [*The tragic truth about cousin marriages: They can cause a litany of genetic illnesses and they're a key factor in the deaths of two children a week in Britain, so why is it taboo to talk about them*, by Sue Reid, *Mail Online*, July 7, 2018].

It's a common belief that Europeans are particularly high in Neanderthal ancestry. So it might seem surprising that Bangladeshis should be so high in this particular form of Neanderthal ancestry.

However, more recent research is revealing that this common belief simply is not accurate. East Asians carry around 30% more Neanderthal DNA than do Europeans [*Neanderthal DNA By Race: Asians Have Closer Link From*

Multiple Breeding Events, Studies Say, by Morgan Windsor, *International Business Times,* February 19, 2015].

South Asians and Europeans are relatively closely related genetically, as has been set out by Frank Salter in his book *On Genetic Interests.* So we should not be surprised to find that they also carry Neanderthal DNA. In this case, of course, the key issue is that they carry DNA from a specific Neanderthal type, and that this impacts their ability to fight-off Covid-19.

So, for the Race Deniers and those who insist race differences in Covid-19 fatality are due to "white privilege" or some other unscientific nonsense, here we have a study in a top quality journal which provides very strong proof that the genetics of race very substantially explains the devastating impact of Covid-19 on South Asians in Western countries.

I conclude with the now-traditional mantra I include in all my Covid-19 articles:

If Covid-19 is not an Equal Opportunity disease, that means our race-denying Ruling Class is frightening most people too much—and not warning some people enough. This will not merely cause unnecessary chaos— it will cost lives.

It's almost as if the lockdown was completely unnecessary for all but elderly and seriously sick white people. It's almost as if, for the vast majority of Westerners, this has all been, well, pointless.

Yes, the lockdowns have been as pointless as race denial, but serving the same New World Order agenda.

The World's Oldest Calendar

Archaeology has been, since the post-World War II period, biased against seeing the Northern European people in pre-history as having made any significant scientific advances at all. They were savages compared to the enlightened south. But that bigotry was always a problem, given that Stonehenge was constructed as an astronomical observatory, and the massive megaliths were moved about 180 miles from the origin site to where the stones are today. Without modern machinery this was a great feat of primitive engineering and manpower, so much so that popular books like Erich Von Daniken's *Chariots of the Gods?* (1968), hypothesised that it was the work of an extra-terrestrial civilisation! Why such an advanced civilisation would bother moving rocks, rather than introduce the people to high tech, is a mystery.

This story dates back a few years, but is worth repeating. The world's oldest calendar was found in a field at Crathes Castle in Aberdeenshire, Scotland.

The calendar consists of 12 pits which model the phase of the moon and tracks lunar months. They date from 8,000 BC. What is also significant, is that the site is aligned on the Midwinter sunrise, also supporting the hypothesis of the site being a calendar. It was possible to correct for the seasonal drift of the lunar year, which the Nordics at the time achieved 5,000 years before this was done in the Middle East. Source: *Endeavour*, October, 2013, p. 9.

Professor Vince Gaffney analysed the site in a paper in *Internet Archaeology*:

https://intarch.ac.uk/journal/issue34/gaffney_index.html

Indo-Europeans,
the Nomads of the Steppes

In his paper "Indo-Europeans were the Most Historically Significant Nomads of the steppes," *Cliodynamics*, vol. 4, 2013, pp. 30-43, Ricardo Duchesne gives us a fascinating glimpse at European pre-history. The Indo-Europeans were a pastoral people who originated from the Pontic Caspian steppes, and in the fourth millennium BC, culturally colonised Europe through their use of what at the time was advanced technology, such as the domestication of horses, the use of wheeled vehicles and the invention of chariots.

His paper compares and contrasts, the Indo-Europeans to the non-Indo-European nomads, such as the Scythians, Sogdians, Turks, and Huns. These nomads did not engage in cultural colonisation, but settled for trade and perhaps a spot of conquest. The Indo-Europeans, "organized as war bands bound together by oaths of aristocratic loyalty and fraternity, they thoroughly colonized Europe with their original pastoral package of wheel vehicles, horse-riding, and chariots, combined with the 'secondary-products revolution.'" What is even more interesting is the social structure of these war bands, which was probably the secret ingredient leading to their success:

"Indo-Europeans were uniquely ruled by a class of free aristocrats grouped into war-bands that were egalitarian within rather than ruled by autocrats. These bands were contractual associations of peers operating outside strictly kin ties, initiated by any powerful individual on the merits of his martial abilities. The relation between the chief and his followers was personal and based on mutual agreement: the followers would volunteer to be bound to the leader by oaths of loyalty wherein they would promise to assist him while the leader would promise to reward them from successful raids. Indo-Europeans prized heroic warriors striving for individual fame and recognition, often with a 'berserker' style of warfare. This aristocratic culture was the primordial source sustaining the unparalleled cultural creativity and territorial expansionism of Western civilization. The Iliad, Beowulf, The Song of Roland, including such Irish, Icelandic and Germanic Sagas as Lebor na hUidre, Njals Saga, Gisla Saga Sursonnar, The Nibelungenlied recount the heroic deeds and fame of aristocrats. These are the earliest voices from the dawn of Western civilization.

Duchesne goes on to argue that this was also the raw germ leading to the rise of the West:

> In my book, I argue that the West has always been in a state of divergence from the rest of the world's cultures, characterized by persistent creativity from ancient to modern times across all fields of human thought and action. Within every generation one finds individuals searching for new worlds, new religious visions, and new styles of painting, architecture, music, science, philosophy, and literature—in comparative contrast to the non-Western world where cultural outlooks tended to persist for long periods with only slight variations and revisions. Using Charles Murray's, *Human Accomplishment, Pursuit of Excellence in the Arts and*

Sciences, 800 BC to 1950, I point out, for example, that ninety-seven percent of accomplishment in the sciences occurred in Europe and North America from 800 BC to 1950. In a subsequent publication, I note that around ninety-five percent of all explorers in history were European (2012). It is my claim that the ultimate roots of this creativity should be traced back to the aristocratic warlike culture of the Indo-Europeans.

Starting from their homelands in present-day Ukraine, the IEs successfully colonized the entire European continent retaining while civilizing their elemental aristocratic ways. During the course of their migratory movements they exhibited a variety of cultural and linguistic forms, including the Yamnaya culture (3400-2300), which spread across the Caspian region and moved into the Danube region; followed by the Corded Ware or Battle Axe culture, which extended itself across northern Europe from the Ukraine to Belgium after 3000BC; followed by the Bell-Beaker culture, which grew within Europe and spread further westwards into Spain and northwards into England and Ireland between 2800-1800BC.5 The Indo-Europeans also spread eastwards across the steppes as far as the Tarim Basin in present-day Xinjiang, China. While these groups did have important influences on Chinese ancient culture, they were eventually absorbed by other non-IE cultures. The ones who migrated into the Greek mainland went on to create the first Indo-European 'civilization': Mycenae. The Mycenaean warriors comprised the background to archaic and classical Greece. The Macedonians rejuvenated the martial virtues of Greece after the debilitating Peloponnesian War, and went on to conquer Persia and create the basis for the intellectual harvest of Alexandrian Greece. The third barbarian Indo-Europeans who developed a civilization were the early Romans who founded an aristocratic republic, preserved the legacy of Greece, and cultivated their own Latin tradition. The fourth were the Celtic-Germanic peoples who interacted for some centuries with the Romans, and then continued the Western legacy. Despite the eventual decline of classical Greece, the stagnation and break-up of the Hellenistic Kingdoms (out of the Western cultural orbit), and the aging despotism of Imperial Rome, the dynamic spirit of the West was sustained several times over thanks to the infusion of new sources of aristocratic peoples brought on by fresh waves of barbarians."

Reading this fascinating history, I wondered where this will lead to now. Has the genetic racial vitality of the West been totally destroyed and we are just in motion because of the momentum of the past, or is there still a vital Faustian spirit there, that will grow into a new civilisation, once this one collapses, as it will inevitably do? Probably not; it will all go to genetic dust.

IQ and the Materialist Theory of Mind

One of the holy grails of the contemporary racial realist camp, a popular version appearing in the journal, American Renaissance, is that IQ is relatively fixed, and hardwired. Whites are smarter than Blacks, and East Asians, well they have IQs off the charts. Another group is even higher. The Left has been critical of this thesis at least since the 1960s, but its efforts have mainly been on attacking the thesis that Whites have higher IQs than Blacks. There has not been much done on questioning the legitimacy of the models of mind employed by the IQ. The neurological assumption is that the brain is not plastic, and that cognitive abilities are relatively fixed.

That is challenged by contemporary work in neurology. David Perkins in *Outsmarting IQ: The Emerging Science of Learnable Intelligence*, (Free Press, New York, 1995), and also summarised by Norman Doidge, *The Brain that Changes Itself*, (Penguin, 2007), show that the brain is not genetically fixed, but exhibits neuroplasticity, to such a degree that it is capable of reworking itself to cope with many brain injuries, by literally remaking itself. This includes stroke victims and a woman who was born with half a brain, but the brain rewired itself.

Even more remarkable is the issue of whether a brain is necessary at all, metaphorically raised in a 1980 paper in Science journal:

https://science.sciencemag.org/content/210/4475/12 32

https://link.springer.com/article/10.1007/s13752- 015-0219-x

"The philosopher Ludwig Wittgenstein chose as his prime exemplar of certainty the fact that the skulls of normal people are filled with neural tissue, not sawdust. In 1980 the British pediatrician John Lorber reported that some normal adults, apparently cured of childhood hydrocephaly, had no more than 5 % of the volume of normal brain tissue. While initially disbelieved, Lorber's observations have since been independently confirmed by clinicians in France and Brazil. Thus Wittgenstein's certainty has become uncertain. Furthermore, the paradox that the human brain's information content (memory) appears to exceed the storage capacity of even normal-sized brains, requires resolution. This article is one of a series on disparities between brain size and its assumed information content, as seen in cases of savant syndrome, microcephaly, and hydrocephaly, and with special reference to the Victorian era views of Conan Doyle, Samuel Butler, and Darwin's research associate, George Romanes. The articles argue that, albeit unlikely, the scope of explanations must not exclude extracorporeal information storage."

The paper goes on to argue that a materialist account of mind runs into major difficulties, being cognitively limited, and thus unable to account for various cognitive abilities.

https://www.newdawnmagazine.com/articles/is-the-brain-really-necessary-the-answer-seems-to-be-a-no-brainer

This is what we're told: Your brain is where your mind, consciousness and personality reside. "Reductionism," noted the English writer & philosopher Colin Wilson, is the "simple theory that tries to explain the mind in terms of physical mechanisms." Thus, consciousness "is a mechanism of the brain and nervous system."

Put another way: Our mind, our consciousness, our awareness and our personality all come from the brain's chemical and electrical machinery. When the brain works our 'mind' is its product. And when the brain stops working we simple cease to be. That's the standard scientific presentation.

The opposing view is we have a 'soul', a conscious self-awareness that uses the body and brain to gather and process information. When the brain stops working the 'soul' leaves the body to continue its existence in a so-called 'afterworld'.

Thanks to modern CAT scans, scientists can see inside people's heads and view their brains, with some surprising results. The results don't prove we have a 'soul' but certainly reveals there is something very wrong with the mechanistic theory that "mind is a function of brain."

There are people with 9/10ths of their brain cells replaced with water, and they still function normally. ... On the left, the dark area in the CAT scan is water (cerebrospinal fluid) and on the right is a normal brain. The horrifying photo to the right shows mother and her child with hydrocephalus. In babies, who have a soft skull, excess water in the brain can result in hugely inflated skulls. In adults the same process results in a brain that is squashed against the side of the rigid skull (as in the CAT scan). In some cases less than 10% of brain remains, yet these people often continue to function normally.

We are told or presume this is impossible because the image (on page 37 of the print magazine) shows the areas in which various functions of the mind take place. The second image illustrates the way electrical and chemical impulses turn the brain into our mind allowing us to think, to have memories and to function in our daily lives. But it appears there is something wrong with this concept... Well, maybe not wrong but inadequate.

The CAT scan image of the water filled skull belongs to 44-year-old French civil servant (proving, I guess the old adage, that civil servants are often brainless) who is married, has two children and lives a normal life. Another case often cited in the literature is of a man with a brain weight of between 50 and 150 grams – normal brain weight is 1,500 grams – who has a first class honours degree in mathematics and a tested IQ of 126. This man was documented by neurologist Dr. John Lorber who ran the spinal bifida unit at Sheffield Hospital. He studied 600 people who had this condition. Some had 'only' between 50 and 70% of their brains replaced by fluid, some between 70 and 90% replaced fluid, and there were 60 people who had 95% of their brains replaced by fluid. Of the last group, half had an IQ of over 100 (which is considered the mean average for intelligence).

There are enough cases of, for all intents and purposes, average people who have their head filled with water not normal 'grey cells'. This is a challenge to the accepted theory that mind, personality and consciousness are the result of chemical and electrical activity between 'grey matter' in the brain.

Perhaps the idea that our personality rests in our heart or liver has something going for it? Aristotle believed the brain just served to cool the blood.

The IQ fetishism of *American Renaissance* and like researchers such as Richard Lynn, is explicitly based upon a materialist theory of mind. But there is evidence that such a theory cannot account for existing cognitive capacities, led alone place some limitation upon human intelligence. In any case, neuroplasticity, and the research cited by Perkins, finishes off the East Asian IQ superiority hypothesis, or any other superiority hypothesis as such.

The *reductio ad absurdum* is the claim that sub-Saharan African have an IQ at the mentally defect level. I have said before that this claim is totally absurd. I spent time in Africa, and did not observe this, and if this was true, the people would have become extinct long ago. So, there must be something fundamentally methodologically incoherent with IQ, as other have shown mathematically:

https://www.sciencedirect.com/science/article/abs/p ii/016517657990212X#:~:text=Abstract%20Arrow%27s%20 Impossibility%20Theorem%20is%20applied%20to%20th e,condition.%20IQ%20scores%20have%20no%20place%2 0in%20economics.

"Arrow's Impossibility Theorem is applied to the problem of measuring IQ. It is necessary to combine specific ability orderings into a general intelligence ranking, but this is impossible without infringing one desirable condition. IQ scores have no place in economics."

The Dark Age: Kali Yuga

Going through my pile of papers, in the never ending paper wars, I came across a photocopy from the ancient Hindu text, Visnu Purana, which was composed at an unknown date, anywhere from 1st millennium BC to early 2nd millennium AD. The writers described the Kali Yuga, a type of Dark Age. They could well be describing our time:

"Outcastes and barbarians will be masters ... these will be contemporary rulers [of this age] reigning over the earth: kings [rulers] of violent temper ... They will seize upon the property of their subjects; they will be of limited power and will for the most part rapidly rise and fall; their lives will be short, their desires insatiable, and they will display but little piety. The people of various countries intermingling with them will follow their example ... the prevailing caste will ... abandon agriculture and commerce and gain a livelihood by servitude or the exercise of mechanical arts ... instead of protecting will plunder their subjects; and under the pretext of levying customs will rob merchants of their property ...Wealth and piety will decrease day by day until the whole world will be wholly depraved. Then property alone will confer rank; wealth will be the only source of devotion; passion will be the sole bond of union between the sexes; falsehood will be the only means of success in litigation ."

The ancient writers could just as easily be describing our world, which shows that the collapse of civilisations has a commonality. We must be close now, given the desperate urgency the elites have to push through their agenda.

Europeans Discovered America Long Before the Asiatic-Amerindians

This dates back a few years, but I have not previously covered it: Europeans discovered America first:

https://www.independent.co.uk/news/world/americ as/new-evidence-suggests-stone-age-hunters-europe-discovered-america-7447152.html

"New archaeological evidence suggests that America was first discovered by Stone Age people from Europe – 10,000 years before the Siberian-originating ancestors of the American Indians set foot in the New World.

A remarkable series of several dozen European-style stone tools, dating back between 19,000 and 26,000 years, have been discovered at six locations along the US east coast. Three of the sites are on the Delmarva Peninsular in Maryland, discovered by archaeologist Dr Darrin Lowery of the University of Delaware. One is in Pennsylvania and another in Virginia. A sixth was discovered by scallop-dredging fishermen on the seabed 60 miles from the Virginian coast on what, in prehistoric times, would have been dry land.

The new discoveries are among the most important archaeological breakthroughs for several decades - and are set to add substantially to our understanding of humanity's spread around the globe.

The similarity between other later east coast US and European Stone Age stone tool technologies has been noted before. But all the US European-style tools, unearthed before the discovery or dating of the recently found or dated US east coast sites, were from around 15,000 years ago - long after Stone Age Europeans (the Solutrean cultures of France and Iberia) had ceased making such artefacts. Most archaeologists had therefore rejected any possibility of a connection. But the newly-discovered and recently-dated early Maryland and other US east coast Stone Age tools are from between 26,000 and 19,000 years ago - and are therefore contemporary with the virtually identical western European material.

What's more, chemical analysis carried out last year on a European-style stone knife found in Virginia back in 1971 revealed that it was made of French-originating flint.

Professor Dennis Stanford, of the Smithsonian Institution in Washington DC, and Professor Bruce Bradley of the University of Exeter, the two leading archaeologists who have analysed all the evidence, are proposing that Stone Age people from Western Europe migrated to North America at the height of the Ice Age by travelling (over the ice surface and/or by boat) along the edge of the frozen northern part of the Atlantic. They are presenting their detailed evidence in a new book - Across Atlantic Ice – published this month.

At the peak of the Ice Age, around three million square miles of the North Atlantic was covered in thick ice for all or part of the year.

However, the seasonally shifting zone where the ice ended and the open ocean began would have been extremely rich in food resources – migrating seals, sea birds, fish and the now-extinct northern hemisphere penguin-like species, the great auk.

Another key argument for Stanford and Bradley's proposal is the complete absence of any human activity in north-east Siberia and Alaska prior to around 15,500 years ago. If the Maryland and other east coast people of 26,000 to 19,000 years ago had come from Asia, not

Europe, early material, dating from before 19,000 years ago, should have turned up in those two northern areas, but none have been found.

Although Solutrean Europeans may well have been the first Americans, they had a major disadvantage compared to the Asian-originating Indians who entered the New World via the Bering Straits or along the Aleutian Islands chain after 15,500 years ago.

Whereas the Solutreans had only had a 4500 year long 'Ice Age' window to carry out their migratory activity, the Asian-originating Indians had some 15,000 years to do it. What's more, the latter two-thirds of that 15 millennia long period was climatologically much more favourable and substantially larger numbers of Asians were therefore able to migrate.

As a result of these factors the Solutrean (European originating) Native Americans were either partly absorbed by the newcomers or were substantially obliterated by them either physically or through competition for resources.

Some genetic markers for Stone Age western Europeans simply don't exist in north- east Asia – but they do in tiny quantities among some north American Indian groups. Scientific tests on ancient DNA extracted from 8000 year old skeletons from Florida have revealed a high level of a key probable European-originating genetic marker. There are also a tiny number of isolated Native American groups whose languages appear not to be related in any way to Asian-originating American Indian peoples.

But the greatest amount of evidence is likely to come from under the ocean – for most of the areas where the Solutreans would have stepped off the Ice onto dry land are now up to 100 miles out to sea."

Thus, the Solutrean hypothesis, long rejected by the establishment because of the anti-European bias of the new class, turns out to be true!

Friendship and Natural Selection

According to a paper by N. Christakis and J. H. Fowler, "Friendship and Natural Selection," Proceedings of the National Academy of Sciences, vo. 111, 2014, pp. 10796-10801, there is a genetic basis to friendships, with ties not only being to similar people, refuting the ideology that opposites attract, but this similarity goes as deep as the genes:

https://www.pnas.org/content/111/Supplement_3/10796

https://www.livescience.com/45674-genetic-match-marriage.html#:~:text=The%20chance%20that%20it%20leads%20to%20wedding%20bells,whose%20genetic%20profile%20shares%20similarities%20with%20their%20own.

"More than any other species, humans form social ties to individuals who are neither kin nor mates, and these ties tend to be with similar people. Here, we show that this similarity extends to genotypes. Across the whole genome, friends' genotypes at the single nucleotide polymorphism level tend to be positively correlated (homophilic). In fact, the increase in similarity relative to strangers is at the level of fourth cousins. However, certain genotypes are also negatively correlated (heterophilic) in friends. And the degree of correlation in genotypes can be used to create a "friendship score" that predicts the existence of friendship ties in a hold-out sample. A focused gene-set analysis indicates that some of the overall correlation in genotypes can be explained by specific systems; for example, an olfactory gene set is homophilic and an immune system gene set is heterophilic, suggesting that these systems may play a role in the formation or maintenance of friendship ties. Friends may be a kind of "functional kin." Finally, homophilic genotypes exhibit significantly higher measures of positive selection, suggesting that, on average, they may yield a synergistic fitness advantage that has been helping to drive recent human evolution."

I put it like this: that in general, friends are part of our racial family or tribe. Humans can recognise individuals of their own race much better than individuals of other races: E. A. Phelps, "Faces and Races in the Brain," *Nature Neuroscience*, vol. 4, 2001, pp. 775-776; E. A. Phelps and L. A. Thomas, "Race, Behaviour, and the Brain: The Role of Neuroimaging in Understanding Complex Social Behaviors," *Political Psychology*, vol. 24, 2003, pp. 747-758.

All the more reason to oppose mass swamping by immigration, which transfers once familiar social landscapes, into alienated deserts.

Nordic Archaeology:
The Nebra Sky Disc

In 1999 two treasure hunters in a small town in East Germany's Saxony-Anhalt, discovered a small disc which has the earlies known depiction of the cosmos, with images of the sun, a crescent moon, and 32 stars. This first depiction of the cosmos was not from the Middle East, the so-called cradle of civilisation for establishment archaeology, but on a hill called Mittelberg, near the town of Nebra. The disc was adequate for predicting moon phases for Bronze Age people, and is regarded as one of the most important archaeological finds of the 20th century.

It is further evidence that Northern Europeans in prehistory were not the savage barbarians that the establishment like to depict them as.

The disc contains gold all the way from Cornwall:

https://www.plymouthherald.co.uk/news/local-news/1million-sky-disc-nebra-contains-2631272

Some think that the disc is younger, dating from the Iron Age, but even so, it is still a remarkable discovery;

https://www.ancient-origins.net/ancient-technology/secrets-nebra-sky-disc-001526

Race and the Fall of the Roman Empire: Lessons for Today

With the American empire now set to fall, quickly, the population largely dumbed down to Joe Biden level of intelligence, it is appropriate in this series of articles to consider the fall of Rome, and especially from a racial angle, which is now taboo.

In a classic paper "Race Mixture in the Roman Empire," *American Historical Review*, vol. 21, 1916, Professor Tenney Frank argued that ancient Rome collapsed because the native Nordic stock eventually interbred with slaves and migrants from the east:

https://racialrealism.wordpress.com/2018/03/27/rac e-mixture-in-the-roman-empire/

> But the existence of other forms of "race suicide", so freely gossipped about by writers of the empire, also enters into this question, and here the inscriptions quite fail us. The importance of this consideration must, nevertheless, be kept in mind. Doubtless, as Fustel de Coulanges *(La Cité Antique)* has remarked, it could have been of little importance in the society of the republic so long as the old orthodox faith in ancestral spirits survived, for the happiness of the *manes* depended upon the survival of the family, and this religious incentive probably played the same role in the propagation of the race as the Mosaic injunctions among the Hebrews, which so impressed Tacitus in a more degenerate day of Rome. But religious considerations and customs – which in this matter emanate from the fundamental

instincts that continue the race – were questioned as all else was questioned before Augustus's day. Then the process of diminution began. The significance of this whole question lies in the fact that "race suicide" then, as now, curtailed the stock of the more sophisticated, that is, of the aristocracy and the rich, who were, to a large extent, the native stock. Juvenal, satirist though he is, may be giving a fact of some social importance when he writes that the poor bore all the burdens of family life, while the rich remained childless.

There may lie here – rare phenomenon – an historic parallel of some meaning. The race of the human animal survives by means of instincts that shaped themselves for that purpose long before rational control came into play. Before our day it has only been at Greece and Rome that these impulses have had to face the obstacle of sophistication. There at least the instinct was beaten, and the race went under. The legislation of Augustus and his successors, while aimed at preserving the native stock, was of the myopic kind so usual in social law-making, and, failing to reckon with the real nature of the problem involved, it utterly missed the mark. By combining epigraphical and literary references, a fairly full history of the noble families can be procured, and this reveals a startling inability of such families to perpetuate themselves. We know, for instance, in Caesar's day of forty-five patricians, only one of whom is represented by posterity when Hadrian came to power. The Aemilii, Fabii, Claudii, Manlii, Valerii, and all the rest, with the exception of the Cornelii, have disappeared. Augustus and Claudius raised twenty-five families to the patriciate, and all but six of them disappear before Nerva's reign. Of the families of nearly four hundred senators recorded in 65 A.D. under Nero, all trace of a half is lost by Nerva's day, a generation later. And the records are so full that these statistics may be assumed to represent with a fair degree of accuracy the disappearance of the male stock of the families in question. Of course members of the aristocracy were the chief sufferers from the tyranny of the first century, but this havoc was not all wrought by *delatores* and assassins. The voluntary choice of childlessness accounts largely for the unparalleled condition. This is as far as the records help upon this problem, which, despite the silence, is probably the most important phase of the whole question of the change of race. Be the causes what they may, the rapid decrease of the old aristocracy and the native stock was clearly concomitant with a twofold increase from below: by a more normal birth-rate of the poor, and the constant manumission of slaves."

It is exactly the same set of processes at work here. And the fall and collapse would occur regardless of the native population being Nordic, since the issue is of the socially corrosive effects of ethnic and cultural diversity, which has been shown time and time again to undermine societies.

Of course, the Tenney Frank thesis has been criticised over the years, with objections such as the claim that the foreign population of Rome was small, and mainly Europeans:

https://italianthro.blogspot.com/2011/01/tenney-franks-orientalization-refuted.html

https://www.cambridge.org/core/journals/journal-of-roman-studies/article/decline-of-the-roman-power-in-western-europe-some-modern-explanations1/CA9302EB1C8F2E37438F592D403DBA4E

However, there is considerable evidence of both the decline of the native stock to breed, as today, as well as the influx of migrants from numerous places, other than Europe, as noted by Martin Nilsson, "The Race problem of the Roman Empire," *Hereditas*, vol. 2, 1921:

https://onlinelibrary.wiley.com/doi/pdf/10.1111/j.160 1-5223.1921.tb02635.x

"The bonds of matrimony were slackened, the birth and education of children were felt to be burdensome. In ancient times the parents had a right to expose children whom they did not desire to educate. Where the supply of food is scarce among primitive peoples this may be excused. Among a civilized people, when economic egotism has obliterated the natural feelings of the parents, it is nothing but, legalized infanticide. This stain on ancient culture, however, did not have any considerable influence on the number of the population. Most of the exposed babies were picked up by slave-hunters; they lived, though in the debased condition of slaves. A more important feature was that the educated classes were decimated in this manner. The ancients also knew other less revolting means of checking the birth-rate, the effect of which may safely be supposed to have been much greater. These expedients are often mentioned in, the medical literature of the period, and many seem to have looked on them as some extreme feminists do to-day."

And as for race and immigration, Nilsson says:

> In some cases it is possible to show whence the men came who took the places of the Roman elements of the population. The old Roman nobility had been severely dealt with in the proscriptions at the end of the AUGUSTUS tried earnestly to save what was left, but without succes8. The old families died out in the first century A. D. The correspondents of PLINY the

younger do not bear the old famous names. In their stead prgvincials enter the senate, at first from the most Romanised provinces, Southern Spain (Baetica), South-East France (Gallia Narbonensis), later on from Africa (Tunis), and Asia Minor. The first consuls who originated from Spain appear in the last years of the Republic and were followed by several others during the first ,century A. D., the first consul from Gallia Narbonensis is found in the reign of TIBERIUS, the first from Africa and Syria in the reigns of VESPASIAN and DoMITxaN respectively. From TRAJAN onwards even the emperors were provincials. TRAJAN aid his successor HADRIAN were Spaniards, ANTONINUS PIUS belonged to a Gallic and … SEPTIMIUS SEVBRUS was a native of Africa, his successors were Syrians. It was difficult for a man belonging to the Greek port'ion of the Empire to attain a high position, because a knowledge of Latin and Roman law was needed for this, and such a knowledge was not common in the East, which prided itself on its own ancient culture. Nevertheless after the reign of HADRIAX numbers of Orientals appear in high places; the western world seems almost to be worn out. …

The mixed character of the population of the capital is attested by many ancient authors. We can hardly imagine the extent of the admixture; only Constantinople, the most cosmopolitan city of the world, can give us an idea of it. CICERO calls Rome a city created by the confluence of the nations, four centuries later the emperor CONSTANTIUS wondered at the haste with which all the peoples flowed together to Rome. LUCAN, the poet and friend of NERO, says that Rome was populated not by its own citizens but by the scum of the world. The Oriental element seems to have been very conspicuous. A famous passage in JUVEXAL states that the poet cannot like this Graecised Rome, but the the least part of the scum is composed of

Greeks: the Syrian Oroiites has flowed into the Tiber, with foreign languages and foreign manners. ...

What has been set forth as to this point may convey the impression that an inverted selection took place, and in reality there was something like it. The peoples that had created the ancient culture and the Roman Empire diminished in number, and the gaps were filled up by provincials. This process led to a sinking of the culture, in proportion as the less civilized provincials ousted the old citizens, and lessened the coherence of the Empire, which depended on the people that had created it. ...

For another defence of Tenney Frank's thesis see:

http://www.askelm.com/people/peo011.htm#:~:text=The%20Race%20Change%20in%20Western%20Europe%20Historians%20have,century%20B.C.E.%20and%20the%203%20rd%20century%20C.E.

For material on the destructive impact of diversity upon ancient Rome:

http://www.amerika.org/politics/watch-the-genetic-deterioration-of-rome/

http://www.amerika.org/politics/why-rome-did-not-notice-it-was-falling/

http://www.amerika.org/politics/how-diversity-killed-rome/

As argued at the above site, what fell Rome is now chopping away at Western civilisation, and it is only a matter of time before the great tree falls, unless some black swan event occurs. The US election, all-round, has shown that modern people have become so dumbed down, that they may no longer we able to recognise how dumbed down they are: witness Joe Biden, who does not know ... well .. very little about transcendental numbers ...or what he signs when it is put before him. Just the way the Dark Lords like it, tasty.

http://www.amerika.org/politics/the-dunning-kruger-effect/

The Whiteness of Contemporary America (Not for Much Longer)

It is appropriate to write on this topic, as for all we know, under a Biden, no, Harris, presidency, America will open the floodgates, and become majority non-white in a couple of days. Here is a refutation of the claim that America is simply a genetic melting pot, from the Genetic Literacy Project, which found that the average White American is 98.6 percent European. This is the result of DNA testing by researchers at 23andme and Harvard University on 160,000 people:

https://archive.is/omuDF

> Broadly, the genomic analysis found that on an average the African American genome was 73.2 percent African, 24 percent European and 0.8 percent Native American. Latinos as expected had significantly more Native American ancestry with the average Latino genome being 18 percent Native American, 65.1 percent European and 6.2 percent African.

> With respect to European Americans, the percentages are much more different than African Americans or Latinos, with European American genomes being 98.6 percent European, 0.19 percent African and 0.18 percent Native American. In general, the numbers seem to agree with what one would expect given the history of American colonization by Europeans and their interactions with African and Native Americans.

> Detailed percentages of ancestry in the various geographical regions showed relatively wide variations

in the ancestry which seem to corroborate historical events.

What are the social implications of this study? The title of Carl Zimmer's New York Times article on the research "White? Black? A Murky Distinction Grows Still Murkier," seems to suggest that the genetic data show that racial divides have significantly blurred as populations have mixed

In the United States, there is a long tradition of trying to draw sharp lines between ethnic groups, but our ancestry is a fluid and complex matter.

"We use these terms — white, black, Indian, Latino — and they don't really mean what we think they mean," said Claudio Saunt, a historian at the University of Georgia who was not involved in the study.

Razib Khan at the Unz Review, has a different view however (emphasis his):

What genetics is showing is that in fact white Americans are shockingly European to an incredibly high degree for a population with roots on this continent for 400 years. If we removed all the history that we take for granted we'd be amazed that the indigenous peoples had so little demographic impact, and, that the larger numbers of people of partial African ancestry did not move into the general "white" population.

Steve Sailer, a long time writer on race and ethnicity, also writing at the Unz Review, agrees with Khan, with some quick back–of–the envelope calculations to show how...

...whiteness in modern America turns out to be not very murky at all. These findings of 0.19 percent black and 0.18 percent American Indian are tiny numbers.

Think about your family tree back nine generations ago, which would mostly be in the 1700s. You have 512 slots in your family tree nine generations ago (two to the ninth power). The 23andMe numbers suggest that for the average white American, 1 of your 512 ancestors nine generations ago was black and 1 of 512 was Native American.

Here's another way to think of it. If the average self-identified black is 73.2 percent black and the average self-identified white is 0.19 percent black, then the average black in America is 385 times blacker than the average white. That doesn't seem very murky to me.

It is important to note that the study has several potential biases that should be taken into account such as the socio economic status of those who might have purchased the test and as Carl Zimmer reported in his piece, the fact that people of mixed race are more likely to get the test out of curiosity. Nevertheless, the large sample size lends unique credibility and the trove of data will no doubt continue to yield very interesting results about how the ethnicity of the current American population came to be.

For now the interpretation of blurred racial divides might not be quite accurate, but as Razib Khan points out, it might be a few decades from now (emphasis his).

But, with the rise in intermarriage and a clearly mixed-race Latino population the lines between the races will become blurred genetically more and more. A substantial number of American children today are multiracial, and that fraction looks to increase. If 23andMe did a survey of American genetics 25 years from now I'd be much more amenable to the interpretation that the media is putting on this survey.

Thus we can see why the elites will be frantically moving now on mass immigration and every admixture program under the sun, to finish off Whiteness.

In the West's Darkest Hour
The Victory of Hermann Over the Roman Legions

At this time of the West's darkest hour, where the wind of neglect that was sown, now is reaped as a whirlwind that threatens everything, perhaps it will ease the dark night of the racial soul, to reflect upon victories of the past that were secured against seemingly overwhelming odds.

One of the great victories, against the odds, was that of Arminius (18/17BC - AD 21), also known as Hermann of the Cherusci, who was a chief of the Germanic Cherusci. He was captured as a youth and rose through the Roman ranks to serve as a commander of the Roman auxiliary forces. He had grown concerned about Rome's intention to crush the Germanics, and he journeyed to Germanic territory to organise the disputing tribes into a solid fighting force.

In 9 AD he persuaded his superior, Varus, to send three legions of soldiers under Varus' command to deal with the Germanics. This involved passage into the Teutoburg Forest. But Hermann had organised for the united Germanics to be in the forest, a natural fighting ground for them, and one which severely disadvantaged Roman fighting tactics. Every tree must have been full of Germanic warriors with bows and arrows, and throwing spears. The battle ended with Varus' entire army wiped out, over 20,000 men! Hermann succeeded in driving the Romans out of Germania. This battle is covered in detail by Edward Shepherd Creasy, *Fifteen Decisive Battles of the World* (1899).

Why should our kind have sympathy for Hermann and the survival of the Germanics, since most conservatives see ancient Greece and Rome as setting the foundations of Western civilisation, politics, philosophy, logic and art, indeed, most of culture? For a start, Rome was the globalist Old World Order of that era that embodied most of the ideologies of centralism that we would oppose. This blog puts it neatly, that Rome embraced multiculturalism, multiethnicism, multiracialism, and most of the doctrine's that excite the globalists today:

https://linkyou.blog/barbarians-the-anti-white-idolatry-of-rome/#:~:text=The%20decisive%20victory%20of%20Germanic%20people%2C%20crushing%20three,A%20Germanic-blood%2C%20Roman%20general%20who%20turned%20on%20Rome

> "I believe that Rome and Greece (especially Athens) appeals to these anti-whites for two simple reasons.

> The first is that they aren't really seen as white (and enslaved Germanics and massacred Celts, the epitome of white) but created art, technology and architecture that is of a high-standard that we would recognize as distinctly European; but the second is that the Greco-Roman civilizations harbor much of the origins of the politics in which the anti-whites today hold sacred.

> The most obvious is that Rome and Greece were the ultimate civic nationalists. Vast empires that, specifically

where Western Rome is concerned, considered all of the various ethnic groups who lived within their borders to be one people; to be "Roman". Alexander and his generals LARP'd as the people they conquered ("assimilated"). The Greek civilizations were also much more open to homosexuality; I don't think I need to say any more about that as you all know of the Spartan warriors and such. Another huge point is that Rome was a Republic and Athens literally invented democracy; believed by globalists and all other manner of anti-white today to be the only legitimate type of government. You might say "but the left are against imperialism!" Tell them about a country that doesn't believe in [homosexuality and] democracy and watch what devoted imperialists they become! It is important to note that when these people say "imperialism", what they actually mean is "white supremacy".

To the anti-whites, the Greco-Roman world was "proof" that people of many ethnic groups can be successfully "united" under a banner of civics and proposition, led by "non-whites", whilst maintaining the high-civilization with high technology, bustling cities of beautiful art and architecture and a rich mythology. But the only reason it failed, is for the same reason we don't have utopia right now in our multi-ethnic societies: Racists. Nationalists [screwing] everything up. If only the stubborn Germanics and Celts would've assimilated to Roman culture instead of their petty tribalism! If only Alexander's generals hadn't been such chauvinists seeking to rule their own corners! Everything would've been just fine!

From the academic historian's perspective, Hermann was that racist who ruined everything. He betrayed the glorious Rome to save his own ethnic group; his blood. Something they see as totally pointless.

Along with this, ancient Rome was not feminist, but went too far in the other direction, being more restrictive than radical Islam of today, with women regarded as property, so if they were raped, this was a property, rather than a personal crime. As shown by the Roman Tacitus in *Germania* (98 AD), a critique of decadent Roman society based upon the Germans, no doubt with a bit of romanticism thrown in, women were much more highly regarded in Germania than in Rome, without falling into the trap on the Left side of proto-feminism.

Earnest Sevier Cox said of the significance of Hermann's victory: "Hermann's victory over Rome preserved the race and culture of Germanic people, for had Rome reached the Baltic with the mighty German warriors at her disposal, few there are that would hold that the Scandinavian brood land could have escaped the power of the Roman empire and the mongrelisation that was effected within its borders. Modern civilization hung upon victory for the descendants of the people he preserved are everywhere leaders in civilized culture as we know it. The victory, by preserving the racial brood lands of Scandinavia and Germany, built up a reservoir of men and women of splendid bodies, splendid courage, and splendid energy, who, beginning four centuries after the Battle of the Teutoburg Forest, broke forth upon the Western Roman Empire, subdued it, took possession of Europe and conditioned modern civilization to a development along Teutonic lines. This victory gave to the Anglo-Saxons their prized Bill of Rights and Common Law, inherited from the republican institutions of Old Saxony. It gave to the man on foot the right of way as against the man on horseback. It gave the presumption of innocence to the individual charged with crime, and an early trial for charges made against him."

This theme is pursued in great depth by Charles Kingsley in *The Roman and the Teuton* (1864). The founders of Rome were the genetic descendants of our Indo-European ancestors, and Roman busts and death masks, painted in the exact colours of the person's skin and hair, show Nordic features, such as long skulls, blue or light eyes, light skin and fair or brown hair. Many Romans, such as Plutarch are described as blonde and blue-eyed, as was Galba and Nero. Thus, the original Romans were Nordics, but they ultimately interbred with migrants of other races, and disappeared.

Kingsley saw Rome's racial decline, and descent into decadence, as ruling power elites pursued policies of centralism, hedonistic materialism, and globalism for the time, which destroyed Rome. The Germanic barbarian thus destroyed Rome finally, but it was already decayed from globalism. The germs of the rebirth of the West already lay within Nordic Europe. If Rome had destroyed this, we would not be here now.

Today, the West is in a much darker plight than at Hermann's time, and the contemporary barbarians are not going to rebuild the West, but are openly working to destroy it, as we have seen from the coverage of the American 2020 crisis. Everything once more, hangs by a thread, and men today are nothing compared to the warriors of Hermann's time - these men would see even our toughest guys as women-men. We have big problems, maybe insuperable ones. Hermann, where are you!

Europe, the Birthplace of Mankind, Not Africa!

Europe was the birthplace of the human race, not Africa, contrary to the mainstream Out of Africa ideology. This ideology, used to foster one-worldism, is challenged by two fossil found in Bulgaria and Greece, dated to 7.2 million years ago. This human ancestor, named, *Graecopithecus freybergi*, demonstrates that humans were evolving in Europe 200,000 years before the hominids of Africa. These beings lived on an open savannah, and this led to the evolution of bipedalism, to aid in finding food supplies. The dry and hard vegetation, led to *Graecopithecus* having wide molars with thick enamel.

https://www.telegraph.co.uk/science/2017/05/22/europe-birthplace-mankind-not-africa-scientists-find/

https://journals.plos.org/plosone/article?id=10.1371/journal.pone.0177127

"The split of our own clade from the Panini is undocumented in the fossil record. To fill this gap we investigated the dentognathic morphology of *Graecopithecus freybergi* from Pyrgos Vassilissis (Greece) and cf. *Graecopithecus* sp. from Azmaka (Bulgaria), using new µCT and 3D reconstructions of the two known specimens. Pyrgos Vassilissis and Azmaka are currently dated to the early Messinian at 7.175 Ma and 7.24 Ma. Mainly based on its external preservation and the previously vague dating, *Graecopithecus* is often referred to as nomen dubium. The examination of its previously unknown dental root and pulp canal morphology confirms the taxonomic distinction from the significantly older northern Greek hominine *Ouranopithecus*. Furthermore, it shows features that point to a possible phylogenetic affinity with hominins. *G. freybergi* uniquely shares p4 partial root fusion and a possible canine root reduction with this tribe and therefore, provides intriguing evidence of what could be the oldest known hominin."

Apart from this, a 210,000 year-old skull was discovered in a Greek cave, showing humans in Europe 150,000 years earlier than the establishment thought:

https://phys.org/news/2019-07-oldest-africa-reset-human-migration.html#:~:text=Credit%3A%20Copyright%20Katerina%20Harvati%2C%20Eberhard%20Karls%20University%20of,by%20more%20than%20150%2C000%20years%2C%20researchers%20said%20Wednesday.

https://www.nature.com/articles/s41586-019-1376-z

Naturally, the out-of-Africa crowd dispute this, and as Kuhn has shown, paradigms seldom get refuted, just replaced when their champions age and die, and become fossils, if lucky. And, these extra time periods explain the numerous discoveries that I have covered, such as the world's oldest calendar in Europe, and other achievements, not made in the Middle East. It is time to put to rest the ideology that Europeans are late-starters in human development, as much as it may support agendas such as the Great Replacement.

HIV, Nordics and the Gene CCR5-Delta 32

Going through my race/genetics folder, I came across articles I had kept on the CCR5-Delta 32 gene. Why do this? Well, from my cuttings, CCR5-Delta 32 provides protection against the HIV virus, preventing HIV from entering the cells of the immune system. What is interesting from an ethno-racial perspective, is that the highest levels of this gene are found in Scandinavia with relatively lower levels in the Mediterranean. The gene is found in Europeans, and is rare, or totally absent in other populations, such as East Asians and Africans.

There are various hypotheses about how this HIV immunity gene arose, such as a response of Europeans to the plague, or that people under ancient Roman rule somehow lost their immunity, perhaps because the Romans from their travels introduced a disease that the Nordics carrying CCR5-Delta 32 were highly susceptible to.

https://medicalxpress.com/news/2005-03-biologists-10percent-europeans-safe-hiv.html#:~:text=March%2010%2C%202005%20Biologists%20discover%20why%2010percent%20of,made%20around%2010%25%20of%20Europeans%20resistant%20to%20HIV.

Still, this shows that racial qualities go deeper to the sub-race, in this case Nordic Whites compared to the Mediterranean. So, race is not skin deep.

The Finnish Race

Continuing our anthropology series during this lull before a massive poetical, sorry, political, storm, I consider this interesting piece on the Finnish race, who have special qualities:

https://www.unz.com/gdurocher/the-uniqueness-of-the-finnish-race/

The issue is that most Europeans are thought, by the mainstream, to have descended from three ancestral populations, the European hunter-gatherers, the First Farmers, and groups from the Pontic Steppes:

https://pure.mpg.de/rest/items/item_3008272_2/component/file_3012570/content#:~:text=%20%20%20Titl e%20%20%20Ancient%20Fennoscandian,Created%

But that model does not explain the genetics of populations such as the Finns, Estonians, and Hungarians, who share alleles with East Asian populations:

The Finns, Hungarians, and Estonians are unique in Europe in speaking Finno-Ugric languages. Most European nations speak Indo-European languages, descending from the original language of conquerors hailing from the Pontic Steppe. Genetic studies suggest that Finns are not just uniquely linguistically, but also genetically. Similarly, the Basque are the only other nation in Europe not speaking an Indo-European language and, as I have previously written, their region too appears to be genetically distinct relative to the rest of the French population.

In fact, any East Asian contribution to the Finnish gene pool long predates the Mongols and even the spread of Uralic languages in northern Europe. The scientists estimate that Siberian DNA was present in Finland at least 3,500 years ago."

However, the Finns are clearly phenotypically a Nordic people, and having some shared alleles with East Asian does not seem to have made much of a contribution to their phenotypes. Thus, the highest percentage of natural blondes in the world is in Finland, 80 percent, and blue eyes, 89 percent:

https://www.insidermonkey.com/blog/top-10-countries-that-have-the-most-blondes-and-blue-eyes-as-a-percentage-of-population-605109/?singlepage=1

If the biodiversity of nature is worth preserving, then how much more important is preserving the human biodiversity, especially the world's most endangered sub-species: Nordic/Nordish Whites?

The Metaphysics of the Indo-Europeans

As I go through my anthropology file, I am coming across fascinating material which is just as well, as post-US election it is very much the eye of the storm, and there is not much other news. Still, as many get ready to meet their maker, this is an excellent time for reflection.

I have written about the Indo-Europeans, or Aryans as they used to be called prior to World War II. They are one of the three groups who came to comprise, genetically modern Northern Europeans. This issue has been discussed by L. A. Waddell, *The Makers of Civilization in Race and History*, (1929), and by Roger Pearson, *Early Civilisations of the Nordic Peoples*, (1965). Waddell saw the Indo-Europeans contributing to the Mesopotamian and ancient Egyptian civilisations, something supported more recently by Arthur Kemp, in *The Children of Ra* (2019):

https://ostarapublications.com/product/the-children-of-ra-artistic-historical-and-genetic-evidence-for-ancient-white-egypt/

Dr Pearson in his book, tells the story of how these early Nordic people of the Neolithic Age moved from central and south Germany, southward to the Balkans, to Troy, into Italy, and later, into to what is now Britain, France and Spain. They also moved into China and and in a previous article I covered the recent evidence for "Aryans" in India, as they called it. There are White mummies in China from this period, the Tarim mummies, and in the past I have written on this at this blog, which can be found through the search engine:

https://en.wikipedia.org/wiki/Tarim_mummies

There is evidence that the Buddha may have been a blue-eyed, red bearded "devil":

https://scorpiobarang.wordpress.com/2017/07/13/was-the-buddha-a-blue-eyed-white-guy/

https://www.amazon.com/Martial-Arts-Blue-Eyed-Red-Bearded-Barbarian-ebook/dp/B00N9P5V5M/ref=sr_1_3?dchild=1&keywords=buddha+blue+eyed&qid

The Indo-Europeans also had a racial and colour awareness even then, seen in the creation of the caste system in India. As stated by R. Thapar, *A History of India*, (1966), "The first step in the direction of caste (as distinct from class) was taken when the Aryans treated the Dasas [non-Aryans] as beyond the social pale, probably owing to a fear of the Dasas and the even greater fear that assimilation with them would lead to a loss of Aryan identity. Ostensibly the distinction was largely that of colour, the Dasas being darker and of an alien culture . . . The colour-element of caste was emphasized, throughout this period, and was eventually to become deep-rooted in north-Indian Aryan culture. Initially, therefore, the division was between the Aryans and the non-Aryans." (Quoted from Clark, below)

In a fascinating essay, Edwin Clark covers this ground and more. One of the profound metaphysical orientations of the Indo-Europeans, was an acceptance of the existence of objective truth, realism, and the idea of a cosmic order:

https://www.amren.com/archives/back-issues/november-1996/

The Cosmic Order: It is a widespread feature of early Aryan thought that there exists an objective order that is independent of what we believe or want to believe — in other words, truth. The *Rig Veda* calls this order *rta,* a term that may be linked with the word Arya itself, which seems to mean "noble" in *The Laws of Manu.* The word "Aryan" comes from "Arya" and a number of other Indo-European words seem to be connected — the Greek *arête* (virtue, the quality of acting like a man, from which we derive "aristocracy"); the Latin *ara* (altar) and the name "Arthur". But regardless of the linguistic linkages, the Aryan concept of Cosmic Order contrasts with ideas of the universe found among ancient non-Aryans. For the latter, Cosmic Order is merely the product of will, a creature of magic, and it can change if those who know how to change it wish to do so. If the priests or the divine king did not perform the proper magical rituals, the sun literally would not rise, the Nile would not flood, and food would not grow. In this non-Aryan, magical view of nature, order does not exist as an externally independent and objective arrangement of nature and its functioning.

While early Aryans did believe in and practice magic, theirs was not a world-view in which nature and the universe were dependent on magic. Magic could be used to influence nature (through love potions or ointments to make weapons stronger and the like), but nature itself exists apart from the tricks of the magicians and sorcerers. Indeed, throughout Western history, magicians and sorcerers almost always come from pre-Aryan Mother Goddess figures or from the non-Aryan Orient — from Egypt, Babylonia, or the "Magi" of pre-Aryan Persia from whom we get the word "magic."

Moreover, Indo-European gods are considerably less powerful than the deities adored by the non-Aryans.

William Rapier   **117**

Zeus, Apollo, Odin, Thor, and the rest did not create the universe and are in fact subject to most of its rules. The subordination of Aryan gods to the regularities of the universe itself points toward a deep Indo-European belief in Cosmic Order, a belief that has major philosophical and ethical implications.

It follows from recognition of the Cosmic Order that some things are true and some aren't, no matter what you prefer to think, that some things will always and always have been true or false, regardless of your wishes, and that some things will happen or will not happen, whether you like it or not. Hence, the Greek and Nordic ideas of "Fate" or "Destiny," that some things are beyond the control of the human will and are inevitable because of the very fabric of the universe. The concept of Fate is probably the origin of the principle of causality and the ancestor of such Indo-European ideas as logic, mathematics, philosophy, science, and theology.

While Egyptians and Babylonians collected a great deal of information about mathematics and astronomy and practiced impressive engineering on a grand scale, their "sciences" never had a really scientific basis. Their knowledge existed either as the lore collected by the priests or as the products of practical trial-and-error. Only the Indo-European Greeks actually systematized scientific and mathematical knowledge, and they were able to construct it into a system because the system itself was their concept of a Cosmic Order in which all events and phenomena were related through causality and its inexorable linkages of one event and phenomenon to another.

It is notable that Christian theology itself, as developed under the Scholastic theologians of the Middle Ages and under the influence of rationalistic Greek philosophy, reflects this underlying Indo-European belief, that even God behaves according to certain principles, just as Zeus and Odin did, and it is also interesting that today even Christian fundamentalists who wish to disprove the theory of evolution on behalf of their religious beliefs try to do so through "creation science." Among Indo-Europeans, even religion and the supernatural are subordinate to the ancient Aryan perception of a Cosmic Order that governs the universe from the remotest galaxies to the life-cycles of insects.

"It is no accident," wrote V. Gordon Childe, "that the first great advances towards abstract natural science were made by the Aryan Greeks and the Hindus, not by the Babylonians or the Egyptians, despite their great material resources and their surprising progress in *techniques* — in astronomical observation for example. In the moralization of religion too Aryans have played a prominent role. The first great world religions which addressed their appeal to all men irrespective of race or nationality, Buddhism and Zoroastrianism, were the works of Aryans, propagated in Aryan speech. . . It is certain that the great concept of the Divine Law or Cosmic Order is associated with the first Aryan peoples who emerge upon the stage of history some 3,500 years ago."

It is from the Aryan concept of a Cosmic Order that modern white men derive their mental inclinations both to *universalism,* a tendency to think in terms of generalizations and abstractions that apply universally rather than in terms of the specific, local, and temporary, and to *objectivity,* the tendency to evaluate events and phenomena with reference to the general and the abstract, rather than to judge them subjectively, as they relate to themselves. While these traits account for many of the achievements of European Man, they also, as we shall see, help to explain many of his racial problems in more recent times."

Apart from laying the metaphysical basis of science, the Indo-Europeans also had an ethical foundation which also influenced the creation of the modern West, a result of the idea of a cosmic order, that human actions had consequences:

> Recognition of a Cosmic Order implies that human action has consequences — that you cannot do whatever you please and expect nothing to come of it — and also that sometimes no matter what you do, you will not be able to avoid the consequences of your Fate, what the Greeks and Norsemen respectively called your *moira* or *wyrd*. Thus, the central concept of Greek tragedy is that the tragic hero suffers as a consequence of a "tragic flaw" that may not be the result of his will or intent but that his fate is unavoidable. Oedipus was doomed to commit the sacrileges of patricide and incest through his very virtue, and there are many heroes in Greek mythology that encounter similar fates.

> The ethical implication that Indo-Europeans drew from this belief is not that man should surrender or fecklessly seek to avoid his fate but rather that he should accept it courageously. Achilles in the Iliad knows that he is fated to die young but, as horrid as death is to Achilles, he readily prefers the glory of his brief heroic life to the obscurity of a long and safe existence. By contrast Gilgamesh, in the Mesopotamian epic, seeks only to avoid death and resorts to all sorts of magic and sorcery to prevent it.

In her survey of Norse myth, H.R. Ellis Davidson notes similar connections between fate, Cosmic Order, and the heroism of both Gods and men:

> In spite of this awareness of fate, indeed perhaps because of it, the picture of man's qualities which emerges from the myths is a noble one. The gods are heroic figures, men writ large, who led dangerous, individualistic lives, yet at the same time were part of a

closely-knit small group, with a firm sense of values and certain intense loyalties. They would give up their lives rather than surrender these values, but they would fight on as long as they could, since life was well worth while. Men knew that the gods whom they served could not give them freedom from danger and calamity, and they did not demand that they should. We find in the myths no sense of bitterness at the harshness and unfairness of life, but rather a spirit of heroic resignation: humanity is born to trouble, but courage, adventure, and the wonders of life are matters of thankfulness, to be enjoyed while life is still granted to us. The great gifts of the gods were readiness to face the world as it was, the luck that sustains men in tight places, and the opportunity to win that glory which alone can outlive death.

The Norse gods know that their race and the world are doomed at the final battle of Ragnarok, but they go out to fight and to meet their fate regardless. The concept of the "Last Stand," in which an outnumbered army of Aryan warriors face battle against overwhelming odds, usually without any realistic expectation of victory, recurs throughout Indo-European history and legend — at the battles of Marathon and Thermopylae, Horatius at the Bridge, in the *Song of Roland,* in the Arthurian legends, at Ragnarok itself, or in the fiery climax of *Njal's Saga,* and at the Alamo, Rorke's Drift, and the Little Big Horn.

Indeed, Indo-European scholars have recognized a distinctive Indo-European myth pattern called the "Final Battle." As J.P. Mallory writes, "The epic traditions of a number of Indo-European peoples preserve an account of the 'final battle,' for example, Kurukshetra in the great Indian epic, the Mahabharata; the 'Second Battle of Mag Tured' among the early Irish; Ragnarok among the Norse; and several others."

Moreover, the Indo-European hero, fighting in single combat, often is killed by treachery or trickery concocted by a non-Aryan or un-Aryan "trickster" figure. Thus Achilles is killed by an arrow shot by the Trojan Paris, Hercules is killed by the trickery of a centaur, Theseus is pushed over a cliff from behind, Baldur is killed by the jealous trickery of Loki, Siegfried is killed by the treachery of his own brother-in-law, etc. It is interesting that in the Biblical story of David and Goliath, the latter, a champion of the Aryan Philistines, is killed by the slingshot of David, and in the non-Aryan version recounted in the Old Testament, David's conduct is portrayed as an act of prowess.

The Aryan concept of Cosmic Order is thus closely linked to the scientific and philosophical achievements of Indo-European Man as well as with his ethical ideas, especially with regard to Indo-European military behavior. The concept of Cosmic Order implied an essentially aristocratic obligation to carry out one's duty regardless of the consequences but also a heroic recognition of what the consequences, including death and destruction, might be. While other races and cultures have certainly displayed and idealized courage, heroism, and struggle against odds, none has incorporated these ideals into its fundamental world-view and ethic as fully as Indo-European Man."

I found these observations by Clark, profound and thought-provoking, much better articulated than anything I could produce. He showed that the scientific and metaphysical foundations of the West, were given to us by the Indo-Europeans, along with a genetic heritage. Will all of this be lost this century, for a few senseless slogans? That would be tragedy beyond measure.

A Genetic Map of the British Isles

This study goes back to 2015, the "People of the British Isles Study": S. Leslie (et al.), "The Fine-Scale Genetic Structure of the British Population," *Nature*, vol. 519, 2015, carried out by University College London, and the Murdoch Children' Research Institute. The study found that the British people are still basically living in the same tribes that they were in the 7th century. Prior to the mass migrations of the 20th century, there were distinct groups of genetically similar individuals, geographically close together.

DNA samples were taken from over 2,039 UK people, and compared to the DNA of over 6,000 present day Europeans. It was found that genetically similar individuals were still inhabiting the same regions that their ancestors inhabited at the time of the Anglo-Saxon invasions, indicating a remarkable genetic stability over the last 1,400 years. People in central and southern England had a significant DNA contribution from the Anglo-Saxons, but because of the genetic similarities between Anglo-Saxons and Vikings, it was not possible to separate the Viking genetic contribution.

The study found little Roman DNA in the genetics of the British, suggesting that the Romans came and ruled but did not marry British women.

There was no single "Celtic" genetic group, with Celtic parts such as Scotland, Northern Ireland, Wales and Cornwall, genetically differing from each other.

According to one of the researchers, Professor Bodmer: "What it shows is the extraordinary stability of the British population. Britain hasn't changed much since the year 600." We thus see the genetic makeup of 1,400 years ago.

Destroying this genetic heritage must be an irresistible urge for the dark Satanic Lords of mass migration, for their Great Replacement dream, or nightmare.

How Common are Beautiful Interracial Relationships and Marriage?

Being laid up from surgery to repair a shattered knee from a sporting accident at school, where taking a soccer class, I foolishly tried to out-match the leading Afro-Canadian student, and ended up doing my knee in, I have watched some TV and Netfucks, I think it is called, when I can't do any more articles. I was impressed by the level of interracial pairings in TV shows and advertising, not in any way saying that this is a bad thing, no sir, three bags full sir. But the bias was to portray Nordic white women and Black guys. There was no other real pairs matched, such as Black women and Asian men, or Asian women and Black men, maybe the odd effeminate White dude with a hot Black woman, which seemed really odd. Why would such a woman go for this loser? So why do you think all this is, does it represent reality? I did not know, and soon forgot about it.

Anyway, TV bored and disgusted me for various other reasons, so I got back to writing articles for alor.org blog, what else can I do as an invalid? My wife dropped the next pile of photocopies to go through, on the bed next to the bed pan. I then came across some interesting material on interracialism:

https://counter-currents.com/2018/03/the-war-against-whites-in-advertising/print/

"There is a notable and interesting body of research on interracial relationships and marriages, it is not exhaustive by any means, but we can synthesize the available data to form an accurate view of such relationships. Pew Research 2012 conducted a large study of interracial marriage that provides a considerable amount of data. Since 1980, the total percent of interracial marriages has risen from 3.2% to 8.4%. Of new marriages, the rate rose from 6.7% to 15.1%. In 2010 the most common intermarriage was white/Hispanic, at 43.3%, other mixed at 30.4%, white/Asian at 14.4% and white/black, the *least common*, at 11.9%. Not all interracial relationships, of course, are marriages, but we can use the marriage data to reasonably extrapolate the information to the wider society and relationships.

As of 2010, whites, on average, were the least likely to marry outside of their race, less than 10% of whites intermarry, while Hispanics, blacks, and Asians are all two to three times more likely to intermarry.

In terms of combined median incomes of interracial marriages, black husbands with white wives earned the lowest amount of any other combination. The black husband and white wife combination were also the least educated. Of the interracial combinations, marriages between whites and blacks were found to be the least stable, and the most likely to result in divorce. The divorce rate is higher in *all* interracial marriages for white women relative to a white marriage.

A study of over two million online dating interactions revealed distinct racial preferences between groups. White women responded most frequently to white men, and least frequently to black men. In light of this data it is all the more bizarre that the combination of a white woman with a black man is seen so frequently in advertising."

Hmmmmmmm, now what is going on here? Could the ever-friendly globalist elites be simply trying to increase diversity to make society more vibrant, and overcome the dreaded white racism? Could be, stranger things have happened.

On This, the "Racist" was Right!

Marxist biologist, Stephen Jay Gould, was among other things, a critic of racialism, at least as it related to claims that supported some sort of positive conclusion about Whites. I could not find, for example any work critiquing say East Asian IQ superiority, although he might have written on it, I did not find it.

But one claim he did make in his 1981 book, *The Mismeasure of Man,* was that Samuel Morton, who measured hundreds of human skulls in the 1830s and 1840s, concluding that the brain volume of Europeans was greater than that of Asians and Africans, was a "patchwork of fudging and fingling in the clear interest of controlling a priori convictions." Ok, he was a racist, just doctoring data, the same way we might see today, the Democrats doctoring votes. Only, he was not.

However, Gould did not go back and do an empirical test of this, by remeasuring the skulls, which is what science, rather than ideology, would require. This has now been done though:

https://journals.plos.org/plosbiology/article/file?id=10.1371/journal.pbio.1001071&type=printable

Stephen Jay Gould, the prominent evolutionary biologist and science historian, argued that "unconscious manipulation of data may be a scientific norm" because "scientists are human beings rooted in cultural contexts, not automatons directed toward external truth", a view now popular in social studies of science . In support of his argument Gould presented the case of Samuel George Morton, a 19th-century physician and physical anthropologist famous for his measurements of human skulls. Morton was considered the objectivist of his era, but Gould reanalyzed Morton's data and in his prizewinning book The Mismeasure of Man argued that Morton skewed his data to fit his preconceptions about human variation. Morton is now viewed as a canonical example of scientific misconduct. But did Morton really fudge his data? Are studies of human variation inevitably biased, as per Gould, or are objective accounts attainable, as Morton attempted? We investigated these questions by remeasuring Morton's skulls and reexamining both Morton's and Gould's analyses. Our results resolve this historical controversy, demonstrating that Morton did not manipulate data to support his preconceptions, contra Gould. In fact, the Morton case provides an example of how the scientific method can shield results from cultural biases."

In an article published in all places, *The New York Times*, Gould is hammered, although one would not have expected it from an article entitled: "Scientists Measure the Accuracy of a Racist Claim":

https://www.nytimes.com/2011/06/14/science/14skull.html

"The Penn team finds Morton's results were neither fudged nor influenced by his convictions. They identified and remeasured half of the skulls used in his reports, finding that in only 2 percent of cases did Morton's measurements differ significantly from their own. These errors either were random or gave a larger than accurate volume to African skulls, the reverse of the bias that Dr. Gould imputed to Morton.

"These results falsify the claim that Morton physically mismeasured crania based on his a priori biases," the Pennsylvania team writes.

Dr. Gould did not measure any of the skulls himself but merely did a paper reanalysis of Morton's results. He accused Morton of various subterfuges, like leaving out subgroups to manipulate a group's overall score. When these errors were corrected, Dr. Gould said, "there are no differences to speak of among Morton's races." ... Ralph L. Holloway, an expert on human evolution at Columbia and a co-author of the new study, was less willing to give Dr. Gould benefit of the doubt.

"I just didn't trust Gould," he said. "I had the feeling that his ideological stance was supreme. When the 1996 version of 'The Mismeasure of Man' came and he never even bothered to mention Michael's study, I just felt he was a charlatan."

So, politically correct *New York Times*, your own article says that the so-called "racist" claim is correct! Hang your head!

Items on Nordic Prehistory

It is only worth fighting to preserve something, if that thing is worth preserving in the first place. Thus, I have sought to present evidence, from mainstream sources, of the prehistorical achievements, and indeed existence of Nordic/Northern European peoples.

In 2019, it was reported, that the coffin of Tutankhamun's grandmother was opened, to reveal that she had blonde hair! Nordics in ancient Egypt! I have written about this before.

https://www.dailystar.co.uk/news/world-news/tutankhamun-great-grandmother-coffin-ancient-17215576

> Egyptian noblewoman Tjuyu – who is believed to have died in 1375 BC – is most widely known as being the great-grandmother of legendary pharaoh Tutankhamun.
>
> Her tomb was found in 1905 – 18 years before Tut's – but it has rarely been opened.
>
> In Channel 5 documentary The Nile: Egypt's Great River, historian Bettany Hughes was given the chance to witness such an occasion at the Egyptian Museum in Cairo.
>
> Footage from tonight's episode shows experts lifting the lid off Tjuyu's tomb to reveal her incredibly-well preserved body.
>
> "She's so tiny and so perfect," Bettany exclaims.

The presenter then notices something strange, the "strawberry-blonde" hair of the mummified body.

Ancient Egyptians have historically been portrayed as having brown hair.

But Egyptologist Salima Ikram explained it may not all be as it seems.

"We're not 100% sure [if that is her original hair]," she said.

"But when you use natrons for mummification, it acts like a bleach."

This substance could mean her true hair colour was lightened to give it a blonde-look.

I have not found anything on genetic testing of this, so we can suppose that the hair colour was blonde, but the establishment finds that inconvenient.

On the subject of Nordics and ancient Egypt, beads found in 3,400 year old Nordic graves were made by King Tut's glassmaker, showing that even then, people got around, and the cultural diffusionists are right. How about *Haaretz* as a source?

https://www.haaretz.com/archaeology/kig-tut-beads-found-in-3-400y-old-danish-graves-1.5414758

Wait, here is the title from the article, cut and pasted: "Beads Found in 3,400-year-old Nordic Graves Were Made by King Tut's Glassmaker."

Cobalt glass beads found in Scandinavian Bronze Age tombs reveal trade connections between Egyptians and Mesopotamia 3,400 years ago — and similar religious rituals.

Stunning glass beads found in Danish Bronze Age burials dating to 3400 years ago turn out to have come from ancient Egypt – in fact, from the workshop that made the blue beads buried with the famous boy-king Tutankhamun. The discovery proves that there were established trade routes between the far north and Levant as early as the 13th century BCE.

Twenty-three of the glass beads found in Danish Bronze Age burials by the team of Danish and French archaeologists were blue, a rare color in ancient times.

Here is one for all our Canadian readers: ancient ruins older that the pyramids discovered in Canada. That sounded like false news, but here is your mainstream media source:

https://www.independent.co.uk/news/world/ancient -canada-village-older-pyramids-alisha-gavreau- indigenous-heiltsuk-people-university-victoria- a7931726.html

"Expedition unearths evidence of 14,000-year-old settlement.

An ancient village that is older than the Egyptian pyramids has been discovered in a remote part of Canada

After excavating a settlement on Triquet Island on British Columbia's Central Coast archaeologists dated it to 14,000 years ago, during the last ice age when glaciers covered much of North America.

It was discovered by team searching for evidence that supported the oral histories of the indigenous Heiltsuk people, which told of a sliver of land during the last ice age that never froze.

Legend has it that the Heiltsuk took refuge there during the big freeze.

Alisha Gauvreau, a PhD student at the University of Victoria, worked with members of the Heiltsuk Nation to excavate the site.

Under several metres of earth they discovered a layer of ancient soil that appeared to contain a prehistoric hearth.

Using tweezers they were able to remove flakes of charcoal from it, which were then sent for carbon dating. This established that some of them were 14,000 years old.

"We just sat back and said, 'Holy moly, this is old," Ms Gauvreau told Canadian broadcaster, CTV."

So much for the Middle East as being the cradle of civilisation; much was happening in Europe too, such as the ancient Irish recording an eclipse 5,355 years ago:

https://www.irishcentral.com/roots/history/first-solar-eclipse-in-the-world

It's hard to tell when the first solar eclipse in the world took place but the ancient Irish certainly helped, being among the first to document when it happened.

The Irish have a long and distinguished history with eclipses. Images of the first recorded eclipse were carved into stone cairns at Loughcrew in Meath over 5,000 years ago, but one of the first eclipses, of the common era, was also recorded in Ireland, by an Irish monk on June 29, 512, in the Chronicle of Ireland.

Eclipses were first recorded by the Irish

Our ancient Irish ancestors carved images of an ancient eclipse into giant stones over 5,000 years ago, on November 30, 3340BC to be exact. This is the oldest known recorded solar eclipse in history.

The illustrations are found in the Stone Age "Cairn L," on Carbane West, at Loughcrew, outside Oldcastle, in County Meath. The landscape of rolling hills is littered with Neolithic monuments. Some say that originally there were at least 40 to 50 monuments, but others say the figure was more like 100.

"Cairn L" received a mention in Astronomy Ireland's article: "Irish Recorded Oldest Known Eclipse 5,355 Years Ago." They noted that the Irish Neolithic astronomer priests recorded the events on three stones relating to the eclipse, as seen from that location.

During their research at Loughcrew, Martin Brennan and Jack Roberts discovered that the sun illuminates this chamber on the mornings of Samhain and Imbolc, the ancient Celtic festivals. These important dates lie during the first week of November and the first week of February, the ancient cross-quarter days. Though this may not be the original alignment we are still left with a spectacular display.

The 3340 BC eclipse is the only eclipse that fits out of the 92 solar eclipses in history tracked by Irish archaeo-astronomer expert, Paul Griffin. With none of the technology available to our modern experts, the ancient Irish constructed these complex structures, that not only have endured for more than 5,000 years but were built with such accuracy that they continue to perform their astronomical functions today."

Europeans have existed for much longer than establishment archaeology has thought:

http://www.amerika.org/politics/europeans-have-existed-for-longer-than-previously-thought/

Until recently, *H. sapiens* was thought to have evolved approximately 200,000 years ago in East This estimate was shaped by the discovery in 1967 of the oldest remains attributed to *H. sapiens*, at a site in Ethiopia's Omo Valley. The remains, made up of two skulls (Omo 1 and Omo 2), had initially been dated to

130,000 years ago, but through the application of more-sophisticated dating techniques in 2005, the remains were more accurately dated to 195,000 years ago.

In June 2017, however, all of this changed. A multiyear excavation led by Jean-Jacques Hublin of the Max Planck Institute for Evolutionary Anthropology in Leipzig, Germany, revealed that H. sapiens was present at Jebel Irhoud, Morocco, more than 5,000 km (3,100 miles) away from East Africa (the region many paleontologists call the cradle of humankind). The team unearthed a collection of specimens that was made up of skull fragments and a complete jawbone (both of which were strikingly similar to those of modern human beings) as well as stone tools all of which dated to about 315,000 years ago, more than 100,000 years earlier than the remains found at Omo. Although this discovery has not yet convinced all paleontologists, it suggests that the species could have been widely dispersed throughout North Africa much earlier than they expected and that East Africa might not have been the only cradle.

The idea of one big human species where everyone is basically the same pleases nearly everyone in an egalitarian time; the notion of complex, nuanced, intricate, and ambiguous links makes people feel stupid and confused, so no one will win a book contract or laboratory funding that way.

As a result, the old Out of Africa theory has great legs because it makes careers. It is politically advantageous to talk about how we all came from one point in Africa and this migration was relatively recent; it is political suicide to say that humanity arose in multiple places, far longer ago, and so our narrative is nonsense. The only way these studies have taken root at all is by extremely cautious wording and the fact that most people have no idea of their significance."

"A newly discovered hearth full of ash and charred bone in a cave in modern-day Israel hints that early humans sat around fires as early as 300,000 years ago" before *Homo sapiens* arose in Africa.

...What's more, its position implies some planning went into deciding where to put the fire pit, suggesting whoever built it must have had a certain level of intelligence.

...It's not entirely clear who was cooking at Qesem Cave. A study published about three years ago in the American Journal of Physical Anthropology described teeth found in the cave dating to between 400,000 and 200,000 years ago. The authors speculated the teeth might have belonged to modern humans (*Homo sapiens*), Neanderthals or perhaps a different species, though they noted they couldn't draw a solid conclusion from their evidence."

https://www.nature.com/articles/nature14317

"We generated genome-wide data from 69 Europeans who lived between 8,000–3,000 years ago by enriching ancient DNA libraries for a target set of almost 400,000 polymorphisms. Enrichment of these positions decreases the sequencing required for genome-wide ancient DNA analysis by a median of around 250-fold, allowing us to study an order of magnitude more individuals than previous studies to obtain new insights about the past. We show that the populations of Western and Far Eastern Europe followed opposite trajectories between 8,000–5,000 years ago. At the beginning of the Neolithic period in Europe, ~8,000–7,000 years ago, closely related groups of early farmers appeared in Germany, Hungary and Spain, different from indigenous hunter-gatherers, whereas Russia was inhabited by a distinctive population of hunter-gatherers with high affinity to a ~24,000-year-old Siberian. By ~6,000–5,000 years ago, farmers throughout much of Europe had more hunter-gatherer ancestry than their predecessors, but in Russia, the Yamnaya steppe herders of this time were descended not only from the preceding eastern European hunter-gatherers, but also from a population of Near Eastern ancestry. Western and Eastern Europe came into contact ~4,500 years ago, as the Late Neolithic Corded Ware people from Germany traced ~75% of their ancestry to the Yamnaya, documenting a massive migration into the heartland of Europe from its eastern periphery. This steppe ancestry persisted in all sampled central Europeans until at least ~3,000 years ago, and is ubiquitous in present-day Europeans. These results provide support for a steppe origin of at least some of the Indo-European languages of Europe."

https://sciencenordic.com/ancient-dna-denmark-dna/scandinavians-are-the-earliest-europeans/1410116

An international team of scientists have sequenced the genome of a 37,000-year-old male skeleton found in Kostenki in Russia.

The study, which was recently published in Science, sheds entirely new light on who we are as Europeans.

"From a genetic point of view he's an European," says Professor Eske Willerslev, Director of the Centre for GeoGenetics at the University of Copenhagen, who was involved in the new study, and adds:

"Actually, he is closer to Danes, Swedes, Finns and Russians than to Frenchmen, Spaniards and Germans".

Split happened within a 8.000 year gap.

The Kostenki fossils were excavated in 1954. The photo shows the leader of the expedition, A.N. Rogachev (left) and M.M. Gerasimov.

The new results reveal that the man is the oldest that we know of so far to genetically represent a separate line from the forebears of present-day Asians. This is decisive when it comes to dating one of the most important events in history.

"We can now date the separation time between Asians and Europeans," says Professor Rasmus Nielsen from the University of Copenhagen and the University of California, Berkeley, who was also involved in the study.

He points out that the Kostenki genome sets a line 37,000 years ago. Here the lines must have split, while the 45,000-year-old genome from the recently discovered Ust' Ishim in Siberia sets the limit in the other direction.

This gives the answer to one of the biggest questions in the history of mankind; scientists now know that it is within the 8000 year gap that Europeans and Asians went their separate ways.

Meta-population: sex across populations.

Previously the impression was that our forebears lived in separate populations and had children within the group, instead, Willerslev now paints a very different picture consisting of one large meta-population.

A meta-population consists of several populations which mate with each other.

The meta-population is connected through the neighbour's neighbours, consisting of people who generally resemble each other a lot, but who also have their own unique traits.

"It was a huge, complex network, and not separate branches that lived in isolation," says Willerslev.

He believes the Europeans must have been one enormous meta-population stretching across Europe, the Middle East and Central Asia.

It is possible to follow the genetic trail; all the way from the Kostenki genome, to hunter-gatherers in Siberia 25,000 years ago and farmers 7-8000 years ago in Spain, Luxembourg and Sweden, up to present-day Europeans.

Mixed opinions

A study published in September, led by two professors, Johannes Krause from Eberhard Karl's Universität Tübingen in Germany and David Reich from Harvard University in the US, concluded that present-day Europeans descends from at least three separate groups.

David Reich acknowledges the importance of the new study, but is not convinced that it changes history very much.

"It's wonderful to have the Kostenki genome and it's also important and interesting to find a degree of continuity from the population represented by Kostenki to present-day Europeans," says Reich and adds:

"On the basis of a statistical test or two, it's a pretty far-reaching conclusion as to how our history proceeded. However, It's exciting - if it's true".

https://science.sciencemag.org/content/346/6213/1113.abstract

"The origin of contemporary Europeans remains contentious. We obtained a genome sequence from Kostenki 14 in European Russia dating from 38,700 to 36,200 years ago, one of the oldest fossils of anatomically modern humans from Europe. We find that Kostenki 14 shares a close ancestry with the 24,000-year-old Mal'ta boy from central Siberia, European Mesolithic hunter-gatherers, some contemporary western Siberians, and many Europeans, but not eastern Asians. Additionally, the Kostenki 14 genome shows evidence of shared ancestry with a population basal to all Eurasians that also relates to later European Neolithic farmers. We find that Kostenki 14 contains more Neandertal DNA that is contained in longer tracts than present Europeans. Our findings reveal the timing of divergence of western Eurasians and East Asians to be more than 36,200 years ago and that European genomic structure today dates back to the Upper Paleolithic and derives from a metapopulation that at times stretched from Europe to central Asia."

Scandinavians thus turn out to be the earliest Europeans!

Evidence, even from mainstream sources, once interpreted, is showing that Europeans are indeed an ancient people, and were not the savages drinking blood out of skulls, that they were once portrayed as. There is a Nordic/Northern European heritage, well worth preserving and fighting for, of much more value than transient things like the economy and consumerism. We have a racial identity, equal to any other.

Shocking Racial "Stereotypes"

This story goes back only to 2019:

https://www.dailymail.co.uk/health/article-7555963/Racial-stereotypes-intelligence-start-young-FIVE-study-suggests.html

"Children associate being 'brilliant' with white men, but not black men, a shocking new study suggests.

Researchers surveyed 200 children and found that, regardless of their own race, they linked the stereotype of intelligence with white men much more than white women.

However, by contrast, the stereotype wasn't applied to black men, as black women were seen by the children as smarter.

The New York University team says the findings feed into patterns of stereotypes that discourage children of color and women from pursuing careers like those in science and technology, where being seen as an intelligent person is valued.

'Among adults, gender stereotypes apply differently to men and women depending on their race,' said senior author Dr Andrei Cimpian, an associate professor in NYU's department of psychology.

'That's why it is important to consider how gender and race intersect when examining children's gender stereotypes about intellectual ability.'

For the study, published in the Journal of Social Issues, the team recruited 200 five and six-year-olds from public elementary schools in New York City.

Researchers showed the children photographs of eight pairs of adults - a woman and a man of the same race - in a setting such as a home or office.

The kids were then told one of the two adults was 'really, really smart' and asked to guess which adult was the smart one.

Overall, the results showed that children named the white men in the photographs as the 'smart person' compared to the white women."

https://spssi.onlinelibrary.wiley.com/doi/full/10.1111/josi.12352

Naturally the establishment screams "racism," but even so, the "stereotype" was not applied to Black men, with Black women being perceived as smarter by the children, which would contradict the universal racism hypothesis. Yet a more plausible explanation is that this fits into a pattern of evidence showing that racial awareness is wired into the brain, so for example, babies can distinguish between races, and link the languages:

https://onlinelibrary.wiley.com/doi/abs/10.1002/dev.21851

"Research demonstrates that young infants attend to the indexical characteristics of speakers, including age, gender, and ethnicity, and that the relationship between language and ethnicity is intuitive among older children. However, little research has examined whether infants, within the first year, are sensitive to the co-occurrences of ethnicity and language. In this paper, we demonstrate that by 11 months of age, infants hold language-dependent expectations regarding speaker ethnicity. Specifically, 11-month-old English-learning Caucasian infants looked more to Asian versus Caucasian faces when hearing Cantonese versus English (Studies 1 and 3), but did not look more to Asian versus Caucasian faces when paired with Spanish (Study 2), making it unlikely that they held a general expectation that unfamiliar languages pair with unfamiliar faces. Moreover, infants who had regular exposure to one or more significant non-Caucasian individuals showed this pattern more strongly (Study 3). Given that infants tested were raised in a multilingual metropolitan area—which includes a Caucasian population speaking many languages, but seldom Cantonese, as well as a sizeable Asian population speaking both Cantonese and English—these results are most parsimoniously explained by infants having learned specific language–ethnicity associations based on those individuals they encountered in their environment."

Even more shocking, "infants show racial bias toward members of their own race and against those of other races":

> "Two studies by researchers at the Ontario Institute for Studies in Education (OISE) at the University of Toronto and their collaborators from the US, UK, France and China, show that six- to nine-month-old infants demonstrate racial bias in favour of members of their own race and racial bias against those of other races.
>
> In the first study, "Older but not younger infants associate own-race faces with happy music and other-race faces with sad music", published in Developmental Science, results showed that after six months of age, infants begin to associate own-race faces with happy music and other-race faces with sad music.
>
> In the second study, "Infants rely more on gaze cues from own-race than other-race adults for learning

                              Nordic Survival

under uncertainty", published in Child Development, researchers found that six- to eight-month-old infants were more inclined to learn information from an adult of his or her own race than from an adult of a different race.

(In both studies, infants less than six months of age were not found to show such biases).

Racial bias begins at younger age, without experience with other-race individuals

"The findings of these studies are significant for many reasons," said Dr. Kang Lee, professor at OISE's Jackman Institute of Child Study, a Tier 1 Canada Research Chair and lead author of the studies. "The results show that race-based bias already exists around the second half of a child's first year. This challenges the popular view that race-based bias first emerges only during the preschool years."

Researchers say these findings are also important because they offer a new perspective on the cause of race-based bias.

"When we consider why someone has a racial bias, we often think of negative experiences he or she may have had with other-race individuals. But, these findings suggest that a race-based bias emerges without experience with other-race individuals," said Dr. Naiqi (Gabriel) Xiao, first author of the two papers and postdoctoral fellow at Princeton University.

This can be inferred because prior studies from other labs have indicated that many infants typically experience over 90 per cent own-race faces. Following this pattern, the current studies involved babies who had little to no prior experience with other-race individuals.

https://onlinelibrary.wiley.com/doi/full/10.1111/desc.12537

https://srcd.onlinelibrary.wiley.com/doi/full/10.1111/cdev.12798

The Leftist position on race, advanced by the likes of Stephen Jay Gould, seems to be increasingly undermined by recent research, even in our present woke culture. Just imagine if there was genuine freedom to investigate race and gender issues:

https://link.springer.com/article/10.1007/s40806-018-0152-x

https://www.theoccidentalobserver.net/2019/07/16/study-shows-babies-naturally-distinguish-races-and-easily-link-them-to-languages/

Nordics and the Issue of Blame

The paper by S. Potthoff (et al.), "Cognitive Emotion Regulation and Psychopathology Arcos Cultures: A Comparison between Six European Countries," *Personality and Individual Differences*, vol. 98, 2016, found that Northern Europeans are less likely to blame other people for what happened to themselves than Southern Europeans. Further, they present other evidence indicating that Northern Europeans are more egalitarian than Southern Europeans. There is thus a north/south divide on the issues of individualism and egalitarianism. The problem with this in a ruthlessly competitive multicultural society is that Northern European people are at a strategic disadvantage:

https://www.theoccidentalobserver.net/2016/04/29/ northern-europeans-less-prone-to-blaming-the-other/

The difference in other-blame is particularly interesting in that it is consistent with the idea that Northern Europeans more readily take the point of view of the other when assigning blame. I think this is part of the deep structure of individualism. When Michael Polignano wrote a book titled Taking Our Own Side, he put his finger on a major problem for Western individualists: We tend to take a neutral point of view in moral issues — not biased in our own favor or what's good for our group. We tend to take the point of view of the emotionally disinterested, rational observer, not swayed by personal interest. So we are less likely to blame others for problems and try our best to see the situation from the other person's point of view. ... Individualism implies an equality of interest—that everyone has interests but no one has a privileged moral position—philosopher John Rawls' "veil of ignorance." Arguments on morality therefore must necessarily seek an abstract sense of morality, independent of the interests of any particular individual; group interests have no privileged moral standing at all. As an extreme example, pro-slavery arguments that slavery is good for the nation (common among defenders of slavery in England during the eighteenth century) or for individual Whites but do not attach any moral significance to Blacks as individuals therefore fall on deaf ears.

A morality of disinterest naturally leads to erecting moral ideals that do not reflect the interests of particular people or groups but are intrinsically good. Moral idealism is a powerful tendency in European culture, particularly since the seventeenth century apparent, for example, in the German idealist philosophers and the American transcendentalists. Universalist moral ideals are erected and then steps are taken to achieve the moral vision by changing the world, often accompanied by a great deal of moral fervor. The anti-slavery movement in England in the eighteenth and nineteenth centuries is paradigmatic. This pursuit of moral ideals accounts for some of the dynamism of Western history.

The analogy with the contemporary world is obvious. The entire edifice of Political Correctness is framed as a moral in-group. Every attempt is made to shame and ostracize those who, for example, oppose massive non-White immigration or believe that Europeans, like other peoples, have legitimate interests in defending their territories. Labels such as "racist" function to define moral in-groups."

It seems likely that this is a built-in genetic defect for Northern Europeans that was of evolutionary benefit in the past, outside of multicultural societies, dealing with their kind with the same genetic predispositions, but not of survival value in modernity, surrounded by hostiles. How to deal with this is a vexed problem. Intellectual refutations of pernicious universalistic doctrines will obviously help, appealing to the same rational sense of logic and justice that Nordics have. But, I do see this as a limitation compared to other races, so note that while I defend my sub-race from extinction threats, I am not a racial supremacist, since all ethnic and racial groups have good points and bad points. Basically no-one should feel shame for their race, and loving one's own kind is the exact opposite of racism, because, as least for Northern Europeans, they can empathise with the other, in fact, it is what they do best, against protecting their own kind, which will probably be their undoing.

Religious Belief and Cooperation

This was passed my way by our Aussie guy: B. Raffield (et al.), "Religious Belief and Cooperation: A View from the Viking Age," *Religion, Brain and Behavior*, vol. 9, 2019. The issue is whether socio-political complexity arose from one of two hypotheses. First, is the idea that moralizing high gods who engage in supernatural monitoring, observing and punishing humans for transgressions fostered cooperation and socio-political complexity. The second hypothesis is that of the supernatural punishment hypothesis, that the fear of punishment by non-moralizing high gods, aided the development of socio-political complexity.

These hypotheses were tested by examining pre-Christian Viking society (750-1050 CE). It was found that while the Vikings did believe that they were monitored by supernatural entities, the Norse Gods were not moralizing high gods. They thus conclude that non-moralizing high gods foster socio-political complexity.

Now, this is probably true of pagan Viking society, since the gods were essentially models of Vikings, Jungian archetypes. These gods, like Thor, did not create the world, and in fact are destroyed at the battle of Ragnarok, the final battle between good and evil. They were tribal symbols, and not explanations of the cosmos.

However, looking at ancient Israel, the opposite conclusion would be drawn, for there is a creating, all-powerful God, Yahweh, who is highly moralizing and does punish transgressions. It seems to me that the development of socio-political complexity cannot therefore be generalised, since different cultures come up with different answers.

Common Enemies and
the Dark Side of Friendship

Continuing our "war" on the *New York Times*, our next piece of deconstruction relates to this, another one of their "shocking" revelations:

https://www.nytimes.com/2018/04/16/science/friendship-discrimination.html

Yet researchers who explore the deep nature of friendship admit the bond can have its thorns, bruise spots and pesticide traces.

Take the new evidence that people choose friends who resemble themselves, right down to the moment-to-moment pattern of blood flow in the brain. The tendency toward homophily, toward flocking together with birds of your inner and outer feather, gives rise to a harmonious sense of belonging and shared purpose, to easy laughter and volumes of subtext mutually, wordlessly, joyfully understood.

But homophily, researchers said, is also the basis of tribalism, xenophobia and racism, the urge to "otherize" those who differ from you and your beloved friends in one or more ways.

The impulse can yield absurd results. One recent study from the University of Michigan had subjects stand outside on a cold winter day and read a brief story about a hiker who was described as either a "left-wing, pro-gay-rights Democrat" or a "right-wing, anti-gay-rights Republican."

When asked whether the hypothetical hiker might feel chilly as well, participants were far more likely to say yes if the protagonist's political affiliation agreed with their own. But a political adversary — does that person even have skin, let alone a working set of thermal sensors?

"Why must it be the case that we love our own and hate the other?" Nicholas Christakis of Yale University said. "I have struggled with this, and read and studied a tremendous amount, and I have mostly dispiriting news. It's awful. Xenophobia and in-group bias go hand-in-hand." Game theory models predict it, real-life examples confirm it. "In order to band together, we need a common enemy," Dr. Christakis said.

That would seem to be a big problem for those who hold to the globalism and cosmopolitanism of *The New York Times*, as it is a bio-psychological argument for tribalism. What is their answer? Well the good news is that the out group does not need to be genocided, even if disliked, and that just has to be good news for everybody, even though the Left/antifa will ignore that advice in the 1917-style blood baths to come, when continuing to kill Trumpers. And, the psychological evidence shows that friendships are fragile, which I don't think helps their case at all.

So, we are left here with a basic argument for tribalism, right in the heart of globalism and cosmopolitanism.   How did this ever get through the editorial process? Lift your game, *New York Times*, you guys are giving too much intellectual ammo to our side of politics. Just go back to telling us what divine beings, Beijing Biden and Karma Harris are!

Nordic Eye Color and Disagreeableness

The discussion relates to this interesting paper, on a topic I did not expect to see: E. Gardiner & C. J. Jackson, "Eye Color Predicts Disagreeableness in North Europeans: Support in Favor of Frost (2006)," *Current Psychology*, vol. 29, 2010.

https://link.springer.com/article/10.1007/s12144-009-9070-1

"The current study investigates whether eye color provides a marker of Agreeableness in North Europeans. Extrapolating from Frost's (2006) research uncovering an unusually diverse range of hair and eye color in northern Europe, we tested the hypothesis that light eyed individuals of North European descent would be less agreeable (a personality marker for competitiveness) when compared to their dark eyed counterparts, whereas there would be no such effect for people of European descent in general. The hypothesis was tested in Australia to provide consistent environmental conditions for both groups of people. Results support the hypothesis. Implications and conclusions are discussed."

The hypothesis connecting Nordic eye colour and the psychological characteristic of disagreeableness, relates to the evolutionary past, where sexual selection favoured colour traits, in the harsh northern climates where there was a shortage of males, due to injuries, dying younger, so that women competed for males leading to eye colouring increasing in diversification, and the rarer, light colours may have had a selective advantage. Plausibly enough, the harsh northern environment resulted in increased competitiveness of males, and thus less agreeableness. Thus, it is hypothesised that light-eyed people would be more competitive than dark eyed people.

This hypothesis was based on a sample of 336 university students, testing Northern European's of UK origin, against non-UK White Europeans. A number of personality questionnaires, and Inventories were undertaken. The result was that Northern European eye colour was statistically significantly correlated with the measures of Agreeableness, with light-eyed Europeans, being less agreeable than dark-eyed Europeans.

Now this is my own interpretation, of this material, only. If this is true, it does offer some hope that there could be revolt by the Nordics against the tyranny which we now face, especially the agenda, I believe, to wipe them of the face of the Earth by passive genocide, something I will address in an another paper. Again, note the disclaimer, that is my view, not that of the psychologists, who discuss other implications, mainly to do with future research, but genuine scientific work is out there in the public domain, for anyone to discuss.

And, while on the subject of colour, men and women seem to perceive certain colours differently:

https://lions-talk-science.org/2015/03/30/when-it-comes-to-vision-men-and-women-really-arent-seeing-eye-to-eye/

Previous research has shown that women have a larger color vocabulary — think *periwinkle, azure,* and other color names that are unlikely to be used by men in general conversation. But is this lack of color names the main reason for why men and women "see" color differently?

Israel Abramov, a behavioral neuroscientist at CUNY's Brooklyn College, doesn't think so. He's curious about how wiring in the brain influences our perception of color. Do variations in neural connections explain perceptual differences between men and women?

Three dimensions affect how we visualize color: *hue, saturation,* and *brightness.* Hue is the actual color – red, yellow, green, or blue. Saturation is the deepness of the color: emerald green is more saturated than pastel green. Brightness describes the way a color radiates or reflects light.

Abramov asked men and women to break down the hue of a color and to assign a percentage to the categories red, yellow, green, and blue. The results showed that women were more adept at distinguishing between subtle gradations than were men. This sensitivity was most evident in the middle of the color spectrum. With hues that were mainly yellow or green, women were able to distinguish tiny differences between colors that looked identical to men. In fact, Abramov found that slightly longer wavelengths of light were required for men to see the same hues as women – hues identified as orange by women were seen as more yellow by men.

However, when shown light and dark bars flickering on a screen, men were better than women at seeing the bars. Men were better able to perceive changes in brightness across space, a skill useful for reading a letter on an eye chart or recognizing a face. This effect was increased as the bars narrowed, suggesting that men are more sensitive to fine details and rapid movement than women.

If you've ever been frustrated when choosing a paint color, you're not alone. This task is more difficult for men, who find it harder to distinguish between slight color differences.

These results suggest that the wiring differences in visual areas of the brain contribute to how men and women see differently, regardless of whether a person has an extensive vocabulary of color names. Sensory differences between sexes have been well studied. In the realms of hearing, smell, and taste, women perform better than men at distinguishing between slight differences. Hormone levels may be the basis for these sex differences.

Abramov believes that testosterone expression early in development plays a major role. Differences in testosterone levels promote drastically different organization of the neurons in the visual cortex in men and women. There are more receptors for testosterone in the cerebral cortex (the part of the brain that processes information from the senses) than there are in regions of the brain associated with reproduction.

Men have more testosterone receptors than women, especially in the visual region of the cerebral cortex. The elements of vision that were measured in this study are determined by inputs from these specific sets of neurons in the primary visual cortex, so it makes sense that different numbers of receptors would result in differences in visual perception.

But *why* do men and women perceive color differently? One potential explanation goes all the way back to the hunter-gatherer responsibilities of early nomadic tribes. As hunters, men needed to be able to distinguish between predators and prey from afar. On the other hand, women might have developed better close range vision from the act of foraging and gathering.

I would agree with the foraging hypothesis, since it would be a selective advantage to be able to differentiate between different plants, those that would kill you and those tasty to eat. But, today, it means that there will always be endless arguments at the paint store about the exact shade of paint to paint the bathroom.

No Color Please, We are English!

According to a study by the British future and Centre for English Identity and Politics, only 10 percent of people believe that ethnicity is a determining factor in being "English":

https://www.theguardian.com/society/2019/jun/30/being-english-not-about-colour-say-majority

The number of people who believe that in order to be English you have to be white has halved over the past seven years, with the older generation apparently driving a wider acceptance of people with different ethnic backgrounds.

Just over 10% of people believe that ethnicity is an important determining factor in being English, compared to 20% from a 2012 study, according to British Future and the Centre for English Identity and Politics, which is about to publish its follow-up to the 2012 study, *This Sceptred Isle.*

The biggest change was noted among over-65s, where the importance of whiteness fell from 35% to 16%. The new data could challenge the perception that the 2016 Brexit referendum reflected an increase in xenophobic English identity. The findings suggest that during the time of the Brexit vote, perceptions of English identity were becoming more, rather than less, ethnically inclusive.

A contributing factor to this shift in perceptions is likely to be emergence of examples of English diversity. Gareth Southgate's squad for the 2018 World Cup in

Russia was a prominent example. Southgate described the England squad as a team that represented "modern England". In an ITV interview, he said: "We've spent a bit of time being lost as to what our modern identity is, and I think as a team we represent that modern identity and hopefully people can connect with us."

This was echoed by Sunder Katwala, director of British Future. "An inclusive England may be symbolised by Raheem Sterling and Nikita Parris scoring goals for England, or Moeen Ali taking wickets in the World Cup, but it also reflects the lived reality of who most of us now think of as English."

Other signifiers of English identity saw a smaller change. Previous results showed 56% of participants thought it was important for your parents to have been born in England, and the latest show 48% do – marking a drop of 8%. "There has been an important generational shift in how we think about England and the English," said Katwala. "There has been no doubt that most people who have migrated to England, like my parents, usually felt they were invited to become British but not often to identify as English, too. An increasing number of their children, born in England, have felt they can choose to identify as English as well as British.

If this is to be believed, then English ethnic consciousness among whites has totally disappeared, as 90 percent figures is in the domain of Joe Biden voting patterns. And, we can take a lesson from the utter defeat of the polls predicting that Donald Trump would be smashed by Biden. Who today would be prepared to say to a survey that race and ethnicity are determining factors of Englishness? Who knows what could happen? And, there is another factor counting against this, and that is the eternal claims of racism against White British, which even if partially true, count against this 90 percent hypothesis:

https://metro.co.uk/2020/09/21/the-english-countryside-was-shaped-by-colonialism-why-rural-britain-is-unwelcoming-for-people-of-colour-13273808/

https://edition.cnn.com/2020/10/14/football/racism-in-football-one-year-on-england-bulgaria-spt-intl/index.html

https://en.wikipedia.org/wiki/Racism_in_the_United_Kingdom

https://www.theguardian.com/world/2020/jul/16/racism-in-the-uk-still-rife-say-majority-of-britons

https://www.independent.co.uk/news/uk/home-news/racism-uk-inequality-black-lives-matter-wealth-economic-health-a9567461.html

Really, the establishment, as a matter of logic and consistency cannot have it both ways. If the English have no ethno-racial identity at all, where could racism possibly come from?

Peter Frost on Nordic Hair and Eye Color Diversity

Europeans are the exception to the rule of humans having one hair and eye colour, not only having black hair, but all shades right down to white blonde. Why? Peter Frost addressed this issue, and I will take issue with him:

http://cogweb.ucla.edu/ep/Frost_06.html

Frost rightly rejects the hypotheses such as natural selection to ensure vitamin D reserves, intermixture with Neanderthals, genetic drift, founder effects, and other random processes. His explanation is sexual selection:

> For some, including the geneticist Luigi L. Cavalli-Sforza, the answer is sexual selection. This mode of selection intensifies when males outnumber females among individuals ready to mate, or vice versa. The sex in excess supply has to compete for a mate and resorts to the same strategies that advertisers use to grab attention, such as the use of bright or striking colors.

> In other animals, bright colors are usually due to sexual selection. Sometimes the result may be a "color polymorphism" (see box). A potential mate will respond not simply to a bright color but also to a rare one that stands out from the crowd. By enhancing reproductive success, however, such a color will also become more common and less eye-catching. Sexual attraction will then shift to less common variants, the eventual result being an equilibrium that maximizes color diversity. ...

but why is hair and eye color so much more diverse in Europe than elsewhere? Perhaps because sexual selection was much stronger among ancestral Europeans than in other human populations.

Sexual selection intensifies when the "Operational Sex Ratio" (OSR) ceases to be balanced, i.e., when too many of one sex are competing for too few of the other. To understand why this may have happened in ancestral humans, we can examine the demography of present-day hunter-gatherer bands. Such groups usually develop an OSR imbalance for two reasons: 1) hunting distances are longer and have increased the death rates of young men, typically because game animals are more mobile and/or less numerous per unit of land area; and 2) the cost of providing for a second wife is higher and has reduced the incidence of male polygamy (polygyny), typically because women are procuring less food for themselves through food gathering. As a rule, OSRs are less balanced further away from the equator. In the Temperate Zone, and even more so in the Arctic, game animals roam over larger territories and gatherable food is less available in winter.

The most extreme OSR imbalance occurs among hunting peoples of the "steppe-tundra," where almost all consumable biomass is in the form of highly mobile and spatially concentrated herbivores such as caribou, reindeer, or muskox. On the one hand, men die younger because they have to cover long distances in search of herds, with no alternate food sources. On the other, men are less polygynous because they bear almost the full cost of feeding their families in a habitat that offers women little opportunity for food gathering. With fewer men altogether and even fewer polygynous ones, women have to compete for a limited supply of potential husbands."

This, though, is yet another evolutionary "just so" story, based upon speculation that feels right. How do we know sexual selection occurred? The sexual selection hypothesis requires that the actual characteristics exist first, so that they can be selected by discriminatory sex selection, and from that point natural selection continues. But this does not explain how those different forms arose in the first place. All conventional biology has is random genetic mutations, but Frost has rejected randomness as an explanatory hypothesis.

https://www.academia.edu/9185330/Dr_Rupert_Sheldrake_A_new_science_of_life_Morphic_resonance_and_the_habits_of_nature

My explanation? I am inclined to go with special creation here, that something of beauty was created by the Divine to add some colour into a pretty savage world. That is not science, but to hell with science!

Rabbi Mayer Schiller on Secession and Separation

I have been researching secessionism, the breakup of nations, something proposed on a universal scale by Leopold Kohr, in *The Breakdown of Nations* (1957). Kohr came at this thesis as a "philosophical anarchist," rejecting the "cult of bigness." This led him to see nations as vastly too big to be sustainable, and he thought that a breakup into smaller units would be desirable. However, while I do not have the book, I recall that he had a chapter assessing the likelihood of this happening by voluntary action, and in a chapter with a sentence length reply said: it is not going to happen short of a total collapse. Men will go on destroying each other right until the end. He influenced less pessimistic "small is beautiful" thinkers, such as the ever-readable E. F. Schumacher, author of *Small is Beautiful* (1973), and Kirkpatrick Sale, who all argued for the need to return to human scale. I consider this the sensible wing of environmentalism.

Others come at secession from an ethno-racial perspective, and this brings us close to the political arguments developing in a limited number of circle today, with the likely end of Republicans ever obtaining the presidency again, in the America of open borders and anti-white racism.

Back in February 1995, Rabbi Mayer Schiller wrote on this, and after rejecting ideas such as return to Europe (Europe has the same problem), proposed separation:

https://www.amren.com/news/2010/10/separation_is_t/

> What then remains? Separation. Whites should enter into serious dialogue with black and Hispanic nationalists who seek to establish racially based nations within the territory of the United States.
>
> Opposition to this idea is most likely to come from whites. Many blacks and Hispanics already have a firmly developed racial consciousness, whether instinctual or sophisticated. Many have no interest in the study or practice of European culture, and this is neither wrong nor surprising. What remains to be achieved is a large-scale awakening of racial consciousness among whites, without which no serious dialogue can begin about the mechanics of separation.
>
> Those who are daunted by the prospect of separation should once again consider the alternatives. Current trends will ineluctably reduce whites to minority status, and there is every sign that hostility to Whites and to their culture only grows as non-whites gain numbers and influence. Aside from emigration, the probable outcomes are some kind of violent resolution of racial conflicts or the reduction of whites to a persecuted minority in an increasingly lawless, third-world society. The former would be horrible for all people and the latter would be intolerable for the people whose ancestors built the nation.
>
> At present, the idea of dividing the nation into racial zones seems impossible. (For fairness sake, in the interests of those who wish to continue the grand experiment, there could be a multiracial area. It would be interesting to see how many white liberals would

want to live there.) However, there are still large parts of the country that are predominantly white. They could secede. This seems a wild prospect today, but as we move into the next century the burden of racial redistribution of wealth will become increasingly unbearable, and the spectacle of city after city following the path of Detroit and Washington will continue. Who is to say what the citizens of Montana or North Dakota may decide to do?

Indeed, it need not be whole states that secede. Groups of counties could declare independence from Washington. If these efforts were coordinated to occur at the same time their effect could be very powerful. How would the central government react? Given the size of the country and the notorious mismanagement of third world governments, it may not matter how it reacts.

Of course, none of this can happen without profound change in the hearts of whites and this does not now seem likely. Nevertheless, there is simmering unrest in the land. Given clear thinking and courageous leaders we may be able to move beyond the clichés that now govern us.

Cultural Secession Comes First

In order to lay the groundwork for political separation there must first be a recognition that the present government, media, schools and courts are at war with the beliefs and values of this civilization — indeed, with its very identity. Many Americans already feel this way, though not many have an articulate sense of the racial dimension of the problem. Some see the problem primarily in religious or cultural terms. They are nevertheless allies of any American who wishes for the survival of Western civilization on the continent.

Taken all together, Americans who feel that the nation derailed after the 1950s are a significant percentage. They may even be a majority. Only for so long will they fail to see the racial aspect of the crisis. They may soon awake — but for now they sleep.

Furthermore, so much of our civilization's crisis goes beyond race. As Fr. Tacelli wondered in the previous issue of *American Renaissance,* even if whites were to separate from non-whites would their culture then consist of the likes of Madonna?

In fact, our unwillingness to defend racial identity is linked to a severing of ties to our total civilizational identity as it manifests itself in religion, culture, family, and the norms and manners that Russell Kirk aptly termed, "the unbought graces of life." These graces once imbued us with a sense of honor, dignity, courtesy, and piety. As these were abandoned in post-World War II America, we lost a clear sense of who we are and how we should live. It was this breakdown that led to a weakening of racial awareness.

Until Western Man recovers his ability courageously to assert his own identity, with all that this affirmation would entail, there will be no racial defense. This will involve a personal, familial and eventually communal immersion in the faiths, culture, rituals and manners of the West. It will demand that we shun the vast cultural apparatus of our decadent times in all its manifestations. The first stage of a counter-revolution then, is to believe, live, and teach as men of the West.

As one who has long felt a deep attachment to the various forms of Western faith, culture, and race, the need for a program of peaceful, dignified racial separation seems axiomatic. At the very least one must secede personally from the current chaos of mind and soul, while encouraging communal and eventually political secession as well.

The first step then is psychological separation, recognising that we live in an alien land, and are dispossessed. That was perhaps difficult for Trump voters to do, while they thought that their man ruled the roost, but in the Biden/Harris era of tyranny it will become easier. A separation of red states and blue is probably even more urgent than addressing race issues, since this is something of an emergency. Until the happy time of separation, what I call "'the Great Divorce," we could perhaps embrace Titus Quintius' "Fifth Political Theory," of living in a diaspora: "You cannot bring a corpse back to life. . . That's the premise of the Fifth Political Theory (5PT) with regard to ethnic nationalism. The way forward is not to cling to the nation-state or to try to carve one out of a multi-ethnic imperial state. It is to reorient ourselves towards a diaspora model. The West is becoming de-nationalized. . . If we are to become a minority in what is becoming someone else's country, and we want to continue our Western heritage, we will need to embrace the ur-identity, that of the tribe. Because we are a tribe inside a vast, multi-ethnic superstate that is increasingly foreign to us (and us foreign to it), we are also a diaspora."

All of this is necessary to begin the long journey, of moving away, for the sake of survival. Outside of the ethno-racial issues, patriot universalists, opposed to the New World Order, also seek to rebuild, in one case, the American redoubt by James Wesley, Rawles, involving conservative Christians moving to the states of Idaho, Montana Wyoming, and adjoining portions of eastern Oregon, and eastern Washington:

https://survivalblog.com/redoubt/

Sociologist Albert O. Hirschman in his book Exit, Voice, and Loyalty, identifies the growing libertarian trend of "Exit" strategies, all the way from the individual level up to the level of nation states.

Giordano Bruno identified a trend that has been developing informally for many years: A conscious retrenchment into safe haven states. I strongly recommend this amalgamation, and that it be formalized. I'm calling it The American Redoubt. I further recommend Idaho, Montana, Wyoming, eastern Oregon, and eastern Washington for the *réduit.*

Some might call it a conglomeration, but I like to call it an amalgamation, since that evokes silver. And it will be a Biblically sound and Constitutionally sound silver local currency that will give it unity."

All of his is a step in the right direction, which is, moving away from those who would destroy us, to be free!

https://www.amren.com/news/2019/09/white-separatism-richard-mcculloch-racial-segregation/

Diversity is Not a Strength, but a Weakness: A Reading Guide

The woke multiculturalists proclaim, as something of self-fulfilling thesis, that diversity is "our" greatest strength. This claim is never argued for, but is asserted with religious fervour. However, there is an overwhelming case against it. I am not going to argue first hand against the diversity myth here, but for education purposes, for any students wandering our way, provide an introductory reading guide.

1. T. Dinesen (et al.), "Ethnic Diversity and Social Trust: A Narrative and Meta-Analytical Review," *Annual Review of Political Science*, vol. 23, 2020:

"Does ethnic diversity erode social trust? Continued immigration and corresponding growing ethnic diversity have prompted this essential question for modern societies, but few clear answers have been reached in the sprawling literature. This article reviews the literature on the relationship between ethnic diversity and social trust through a narrative review and a meta-analysis of 1,001 estimates from 87 studies. The review clarifies the core concepts, highlights pertinent debates, and tests core claims from the literature on the relationship between ethnic diversity and social trust. Several results stand out from the meta-analysis. We find a statistically significant negative relationship

between ethnic diversity and social trust across all
The relationship is stronger for trust in neighbors and
when ethnic diversity is measured more locally.
Covariate conditioning generally changes the
relationship only slightly. The review concludes by
discussing avenues for future research."

> 2. Dinesen and K. M. Sonderskov, "Ethnic Diversity
> and Social Trust: Evidence from the Micro-
> Context," *American Sociological Review*, vol. 80,
> 2015:

"We argue that residential exposure to ethnic
diversity reduces social trust. Previous within-country
analyses of the relationship between contextual ethnic
diversity and trust have been conducted at higher levels
of aggregation, thus ignoring substantial variation in
actual exposure to ethnic diversity. In contrast, we
analyze how ethnic diversity of the immediate micro-
context—where interethnic exposure is inevitable—
affects trust. We do this using Danish survey data linked
with register-based data, which enables us to obtain
precise measures of the ethnic diversity of each
individual's residential surroundings. We focus on
contextual diversity within a radius of 80 meters of a
given individual, but we also compare the effect in the
micro-context to the impact of diversity in more
aggregate contexts. Our results show that ethnic
diversity in the micro-context affects trust negatively,
whereas the effect vanishes in larger contextual units.
This supports the conjecture that interethnic exposure
underlies the negative relationship between ethnic
diversity in residential contexts and social trust."

While there are not many papers showing that diversity undermines social trust, the above papers give a comprehensive guide to the technical literature.

For those who need an easier read, not so academic, Brett Stevens at Amerika.org, has been hammering away at the diversity cult for many years, hitting it from so many directions, that at least philosophically, it has long ago hit the canvass:

3. http://www.amerika.org/politics/danish-study-finds-diversity-creates-distrust-closest-to-home/#:~:text=Danish%20study%20finds%20diversity%20creates%20distrust%20closest%20to,this%20study%20limits%20impact%20to%20very%20immediate%20experience%3A

4. http://www.amerika.org/politics/diversity-sabotages-community/

> It [diversity] destroys the civilization around it. As the thesis of Dr. Eitan Adres from the School of Political Sciences at the University of Haifa, reveals, diversity — in addition to genetic and cultural genocide — also destroys any sense of social trust and work toward shared goals. In other words, diversity makes citizens into sociopaths:

> The findings showed that the more people consider themselves to adhere to the values of globalization, consumerism, and individualism, and the more they regard themselves as "citizens of the world" exposed to globalization, the less likely they are to contribute to public goods and the more likely they are to seek to be "free riders" on the contributions of others.

> This finding was particularly apparent in the first experiment, when the participants were divided into groups and received 100 tokens each. The participants

were asked to choose an amount from their 100 tokens to be pooled in a communal pot. The total amount donated would be doubled and this doubled amount would be distributed evenly among all participants, no matter how much each one contributed. Thus each individual received the equal portion of the communal pot together with the tokens they did not contribute to the pot. The collective interest in this situation is that each participant will contribute all their tokens to the collective pot. The individual interest is not to contribute anything, and to add the money shared from the pot to the 100 tokens. The study found that 30 percent of German participants and 25 percent of the Australians preferred to keep all their tokens to themselves. By contrast, only 3.6 percent of the Columbians and 12 percent of the Israelis chose to do so.

5. http://www.amerika.org/politics/diversity-doesnt-work/

6. http://www.amerika.org/science/equality-a-consequence-of-diversity/

7. http://www.amerika.org/politics/aristotle-and-plato-on-why-diversity-is-tyranny/

8. http://www.amerika.org/science/science-confirms-it-diversity-destroys-civilization/

The analysis offered on this site of diversity does not look at the unique traits of groups, only the necessary idea that any group is constituted around a unique values system and in order to defend that, needs to have control over its destiny and the ability to exclude other groups. This means that more than one group in the same area causes social dissolution and civilization collapse.

In fact, for more than twenty-five years, the writers collected here have been pointing out that diversity destroys social order and is dysfunctional as a policy as a result. We cannot make it work because it is paradoxical and therefore will always fail, but will fail slowly, taking our civilization down with it as that society expends all of its resources to try to make an illusion into reality, although tyrants and rioting plebs love it because the perceived goodness of diversity gives them virtually unlimited power.

As if conjured up from our laboratories, confirms that diversity results in conflict (via Heartiste via hbdchick):

However, in countries where ethnicity is more strongly predictive of culture, as captured by a high, violent conflict is more likely, and public goods provision tends to be lower. Our interpretation of this empirical result is that in societies where individuals differ from each other in both ethnicity and culture, social antagonism is greater, and political economy outcomes are worse.

In other words, wherever there are groups that have united genetics to value systems ("culture") there is conflict if more than one occupies a space."

9. http://www.amerika.org/politics/research-confirms-that-diversity-destroys-social-trust/#:~:text=Research%20Confirms%20That%20Diversity%20Destroys%20Social%20Trust%20by,freely%20and%20with%20an%20expectation%20of%20fair%20treatment.

10. http://www.amerika.org/politics/what-asiatic-admixture-looks-like/

11. http://www.amerika.org/politics/why-white-ethnostates-are-inevitable/

12. http://www.amerika.org/politics/black-woman-points-out-that-diversity-is-genocide/

That should do as a start for your research!

On Blondes

Blonde jokes were once the go, all with the punchline that blondes are idiots, along the stereotype of Marilyn Monroe and later sex toys. But, that stereotype conflicts somewhat with the evil blonde stereotype seen in action movies, where the blonde men are the bad guys. Not really credible if blondes are dumb; the blonde bad guys had blonde mothers. But, blondes are not dumb, and anyway, that thesis contradicts the Leftist mantra of no intelligence difference for races/sub-races, and has a genocidal undertone to it.

https://pulptastic.com/blondes-aint-dumb/

https://theconversation.com/are-blondes-actually-dumb-56560

In fact, blondes have complex DNA, with over three times the number of genetic variants than brunettes or redheads:

https://www.dailymail.co.uk/news/article-6563471/Not-dumb-Blonds-complex-DNA-study-says.html#:~:text=%20Blondes%20have%20more%20complex%20DNA%2C%20with%20more,explain%20why%20truly%20blonde%20people%20are...%20More%20

Blondes may have a ditzy reputation, but their lighter locks are far more complex than scientists thought.

For true blonde hair requires some 200 genetic variants – compared with 60 for brown hair and even less for redheads.

In one of the biggest studies of its kind scientists at the Medical Research Council's human genetics unit analysed DNA from 39,397 blonde women and men of European descent.

It was assumed that blonde hair had a basic genetic structure but the finding may explain why truly blonde people are rarer than other colours.

Only 12.7 per cent of women have pure blonde hair, and 9.9 per cent of men.

One theory is that blonde hair evolved at the end of the Ice Age, when females outnumbered males. Blondeness may have developed as a way to stand out.

https://www.researchgate.net/publication/262782873_A_molecular_basis_for_classic_blond_hair_color_in_Europeans

https://www.sciencemag.org/news/2014/06/genetics-blond-hair

Fascinating, but very soon, the research question will be; why did blonde and red hair go extinct, if things do not change.

Covid-1984 and Race Realism

I like Vdare.com, as much as I dislike *American Renaissance*, but I must admit that the later has got better. Have they read my critiques? Who knows? Would they care? Anyway, the issue of Covid-19 having a racial basis is fascinating, and when I first read it, even though people would call me a racist (anyone white writing about race is, they say, so why argue on that point, about a silly word?) I was somewhat skeptical, but the latest piece by Lance Welton, really socks it out of the ball park. Say, has any Yankee footballer ever thrown a football out of the stadium, onto the road outside?

https://vdare.com/articles/covid-19-another-genetic-factor-emerges-race-deniers-furious

The new study—"Racial/Ethnic Variation in Nasal Gene Expression of Transmembrane Serine Protease 2 (TMPRSS2)"—was published in the prestigious journal on September 10th and was carried out by three researchers at the Icahn School of Medicine at Mount Sinai, New York [Supinda Bunyavanich; Chantal Grant, MD; and Alfin Vicencio]. It sets out to make sense of why African-Americans suffer a death rate from Covid-19 that is around three times their proportion of the U.S. population. The researchers tested a sample of 305 people in their local hospital system, the sample being 8.2% Asian, 15.4% Black, 26.6% Latino, 9.5% mixed race/ethnicity, and 40.3% White. Their key finding: the expression of the Transmembrane serine protease 2 (shortened to TMPRSS2) was significantly higher among black individuals than it was in Asian, Latino, mixed race/ethnicity, or white individuals. Why is this important? Covid-19 enters the body via contact with its airways, such as the tissues in the nose. If the TMPRSS2 gene is present in its strong form, then the body will produce high levels of the enzyme. This enzyme, present in the body's tissues, means that the virus is better able to enter the tissues and so spread throughout the body, potentially killing the host. If the host has a high expression of TMPRSS2 in its nasal tissues, then, write the authors, "this activates the SARS-CoV-2 spike protein and cleaves the angiotensin-converting enzyme 2 receptor to which the virus binds, enabling SARS-CoV-2 to enter the body" and also more easily spread. According to the research, blacks expressed TMPRSS2 at a higher rate than Asians. Asians expressed it more than Latinos, Latinos had a higher expression than Mixed race people and these, in turn, had a higher expression than whites.

This means that with regard not just to the ability to synthesise UV Light into Vitamin D, but also with regard to this cause, whites are the best adapted of these races to successfully fight off Covid-19. The nasal tissues of whites are such that, compared to other races, the Corona virus finds it more difficult to penetrate white tissues and spread through white bodies. By contrast, the WuFlu finds it relatively easy to penetrate black tissues and spread through black bodies. As the researchers summarize: Given the essential role of TMPRSS2 in SARS-CoV-2 entry, higher nasal expression of TMPRSS2 may contribute to the higher burden of COVID-19 among Black individuals . . . The finding of racial/ethnic variation in TMPRSS2 expression emphasizes that inclusion of diverse participants and analyses stratified by race/ethnicity should be incorporated into such trials. In plain English, the researchers have demonstrated once again that Covid-19 is not an "equal opportunity" disease and that it disproportionately impacts blacks for genetic reasons, among others. This means that supposedly "privileged" whites should feel no guilt whatsoever about the way in which Covid-19 disproportionately impacts blacks (except in as far as they listened to race-deniers like Dr. Gupta). And it also means that, for all but the least healthy white people, the inconvenience, destruction of liberty and economic disaster brought about by the WuFlu shutdowns has been, essentially, in vain.

It is a Democrat campaign talking point that the U.S. may have the most deaths of any developed country. But this is to be expected when about 40% of the U.S. population are non-whites and these are genetically much more likely to die of Covid-19 than are whites. To criticize the Trump Administration on this basis, as the Democrats are doing, is akin to bemoaning high crime rates in the U.S. without taking into account that blacks are a significant minority in the U.S. and commit crime at roughly the same high rates they do in black-majority countries. One problem with the TMPRSS2 hypothesis: the incidence of Covid-19 in Africa itself is quite low. I first pointed this out in April and it continues to be the case:

https://www.dw.com/en/covid-19-in-africa-milder-than-expected-pandemic-has-experts-puzzled/a-54918467

It's possible that the benefits conferred by blacks' greater ability to absorb vitamin-D in the African climate, combined with their relative absence of life-style diseases like obesity, to which American blacks are particularly prone, simply overwhelm the TMPRSS2 effect. Plus African blacks, under greater selection pressure, may have relatively stronger immune systems.

If true, this raises a problem for the holy hierarchy that *American Renaissance* and other race realists operates with, with the super East Asians always trumping the inferior Whites, who must exist only by some cosmic accident of nature. And, the Covid-19 argument is all based on some of the establishment narrative about Covid-19, but still it is useful since it throws metaphorical salty water into the eyes of the establishment on the race issue, which is always good, until we have the guts to walk away from it all:

https://www.theoccidentalobserver.net/2020/09/25/walk-away-western-man-a-declaration-of-white-independence/

As for an update on race material, for the curious Canadian, here goes:

https://www.takimag.com/article/suicide-on-the-trans-black-express/

https://www.naturalnews.com/2020-09-17-seditious-cdc-moves-forward-critical-race-theory-instruction.html

https://www.unz.com/imercer/ethnocidal-critical-race-theory-is-upon-us-like-white-on-rice/

> This Cultural Marxism of a theory is an ill-founded, purely political, symbolic figment that appeals not to empirical evidence, reason and morality, but to the roiling, base emotions of rage and resentment against anyone with a white face. Say it! A "white" face: The words media conservatives cannot bring themselves to utter. Not even Mr. Rufo. The aforementioned path-blazing investigator into, and crusader against, Critical Race Theory in the U.S. concludes his inquiry thus: "Let me say it plainly: critical race theory is a toxic, pseudoscientific, and racist ideology that is taking over our public institutions—and will be weaponized against the American people." Yet, the only Americans Critical Race Theory targets with ethnocidal animosity are white Americans. That's also the main reason white

women like Jessica Krug and Rachel Dolezal pretend to be black: In America, white is bad and black is beautiful. Contra Tucker Carlson: More than they long to join the "booming racial grievance" industry—as a guest on the Fox News show contended—these pitiful poseurs want to be included in black supremacy's mythology. Like black Americans, these women simply want to be looked upon as carrying the heaviest historic baggage; nobler and more righteous than the rest. The words "preordained and predetermined" are key to understanding Critical Race Theory, according to which power relationships in society are proscribed—and statically fixed for posterity. Consequently, Critical Race Theory always inveighs against whites and for other, more exotic identities.

So how did it get to this level? Well, as always, when one is surrounded by enemies, including most of one's own kind, you give an inch and they take a light year.

https://www.unz.com/proberts/does-western-civilization-have-a-future-or-is-it-already-in-its-grave/

I know a software engineer employed by a private company who had to go to a sensitivity training session where white male employees had to stand up and be identified as oppressors of the female and non-white employees. There are now large numbers of firms whose service is to denigrate white males at mandatory sensitivity-training sessions that are now part of employment obligations at private, government, and government funded companies. Because of the far-reaching popularity of my columns, I receive numerous emails from white male employees describing how much they hate their jobs, because of the hostility of their female and black bosses toward white males. They pray for an Asian boss—Chinese, Japanese, Korean—because they judge them by performance, not by an anti-white male ideology. White bosses are unreliable, because they got to be bosses by being self-hating white males. What I have reported is the facts of today. Yet we hear continually that being white is a privilege. This alleged privilege, if it exists, is very rare. No white male, unless he is self-hating, has white privilege .... Nor at my friend's software company. In her book, *The Blackening of Europe*, Clare Ellis describes the ideas that over the decades deracinated the white European ethnicities of confidence in their race, culture and achievements. This confidence destroying deracination has enabled the ongoing largely unopposed riots and looting in numerous American cities. The white liberals who govern these cities lack the confidence to maintain law and order. They have been convinced that law and order is a white privilege. Whether or not Trump wins re-election, Western Civilization may be in its grave, killed by white liberals and .... from the Frankfurt School imported into America. But if Trump loses re-election fairly, it will be definite proof that the structure of belief that upholds Western civilization has completely collapsed, and white people themselves will have voted their own demise.

This is a hard problem that the economics types just can't see. It transcends the economic system, and all economic tinkering, as economics and finance depends upon a cultural superstructure to function, and that is what is being undermined now. But don't get depressed, for I am working on a solution, day and night. But, it is hard to do with a people who just seem to want to die, as the above article concluded.

The Sport of Raping
White Women in Europe

The only way to make sense of this is that a civilisation has given up on itself and is happy to allow its women and children to be raped, wanting to be cancelled. https://www.breitbart.com/europe/2020/09/27/iraqi-migrants-accused-dragging-women-car-raping-them/

https://www.breitbart.com/europe/2020/09/27/women-in-france-assaulted-wearing-skirts-public/

https://www.breitbart.com/europe/2020/08/05/berlin-police-210-rapes-from-march-to-july-half-of-cases-involve-migrants/

According to statistics released by police in the German capital of Berlin, the city saw 210 rapes between March and July, an average of two rape cases per day. The State Police criminal investigation unit, known in Germany as the Kripo, said that cases of serious rape in Berlin are surging, and of the 210 cases reported between March and July at least 50 of the victims were children below the age of 16. The Kripo also say that around half of the suspects in the rape cases come from a foreign background — far higher than the migrant population of Berlin, which amounts to around 29.9 per cent of the city's total residents, Focus reports. Marcel Luthe, a member of the Free Democratic Party (FDP), commented on the statistics, saying: "The far disproportionate proportion of foreign suspects shows that the causes urgently need to be clarified and discussed transparently. And then effective crime prevention must be pursued.

https://www.breitbart.com/europe/2020/07/26/frei
burg-migrant-gang-rapists-sentenced-german-court/

No doubt this is all part of a generalised Great Replacement plan, but what is being missed here is that ultimately the entire cultural infrastructure of these societies is going to collapse, and the elites will need to flee ... but to where? Only outer space is the option, with the Earth transformed into a diverse battle ground. Good luck with the radiation.

Respect Cultural Diversity!

Cultural diversity, so long as it is not our culture, which the Left tells us daily is only suitable for junking because of Racism Pty Ltd, is wonderful. And who could possible doubt that? Lack of identity is our identity; plurality is our unity, multicult is our culture. Selective cultural relativism, rules. Or so we are told.

https://www.news.com.au/national/south-australia/afghan-man-mustafa-naseri-who-asked-teenager-to-meet-with-him-for-sex-acts-says-age-gap-is-the-norm-in-his-culture/news-story/2f62937604ee243e1b669e11741f6c6b

An Afghan man who groomed a 14-year-old girl for sexual activity explained that, in his culture, an age gap was "the norm" and there was no minimum age for sexual activity. Mustafa Naseri, 21, thought he was speaking with a teenager over the messaging app Kik in March and July last year. However, the recipient of the messages was in reality an undercover police officer posing as a young person. Naseri this week avoided jail, instead placed on a bond after he pleaded guilty to two grooming offences. In the conversations with the girl, he asked her for a photograph and whether she had reached puberty. Naseri, who arrived in Australia in 2008, later asked if she would meet up and engage in a sexual act with him. A meeting was arranged but he was eventually arrested at a railway station in Adelaide. Sentencing him in the District Court, Judge Geraldine Davison said Naseri told police he was from where there is no minimum age for sexual activity. He

said he started the conversations because he felt bored
and lonely.

Yes, that is true, there is no legal age of consent in Afghanistan, because ... surprise, surprise ... sexual activity outside of marriage in Afghanistan is illegal!

https://www.ageofconsent.net/world/afghanistan#:~:text=There%20is%20no%20age%20of,close%2Din%2Dage%20exemption

Now it's Medical Racism!

Whenever I hear of the medical journal *The Lancet*, I think of some kind of basin to collect pus. No, a lancet is actually a fine, sharp pointed needle, used mainly to pinch the skin in blood sugar monitoring. Or, it is part of the fight against racism, the deadliest disease in the world, apparently. Move right over Covid-1984!

https://www.breitbart.com/politics/2020/10/05/woke-lancet-denounces-medical-racism-in-united-states/

https://www.thelancet.com/journals/lancet/article/PIIS0140-6736(20)32032-8/fulltext?dgcid=raven_jbs_etoc_email

The killing of Eric Garner in 2014 at the hands of the New York Police Department and the footage that circulated of his death after he was put in a chokehold elevated the phrase "I can't breathe" to a protest chant for those in the fight against structural racism worldwide. Its repetition by George Floyd in Minneapolis, MN, USA, in 2020 and by others in anti-racism protests amid the COVID-19 pandemic has deepened the salience of these words. While much public health research has shown that racism is a fundamental determinant of health outcomes and disparities, racist policy and practice have also been integral to the historical formation of the medical academy in the USA. The term structural violence has its origins in peace studies in the 1960s as a way of understanding the iniquities of imperialism that persisted in the post-colonial world. As Paul Farmer and colleagues have described, structural violence explains how the organisation of society "puts individuals and populations in harm's way. The arrangements are structural because they are embedded in the political and economic organization of our social world; they are violent because they cause injury to people (typically, not those responsible for perpetuating such inequalities)." While no single concept can capture the complexity or full dynamics of racism, the brief historical examples we discuss here show that structural violence is helpful for understanding how the histories of violence, neglect, and oppression that crisscross law enforcement, politics, medical care, and public health are inextricably linked and manifested in the present. Like the history of US policing, the history of medicine and health care in the USA is marked by racial injustice and myriad forms of violence: unequal access to health care, the segregation of medical facilities, and the exclusion of African Americans from medical education are some of the most obvious examples. These, together with inequalities in housing, employment opportunities, wealth, and social service provision, produce disproportionate health disparities by race. The health community needs to confront these painful histories of structural violence to develop more effective anti-racist and benevolent public health responses to entrenched health inequalities, the COVID-19 pandemic, and future pandemics.

For a medical article, there is no consideration that the arguable real cause of death of Floyd was a drug overdose, as Floyd had a "fatal level" of fentanyl in his system:

https://www.kare11.com/article/news/local/george-floyd/new-court-docs-say-george-floyd-had-fatal-level-of-fentanyl-in-his-system/89-ed69d09d-a9ec-481c-90fe-7acd4ead3d04

What about the other Black mentioned, Eric Garner, was that a police murder? Here, a Staten island grand jury heard the case and decided that charges should not be brought against the officer who used a choke hold to subdue Garner. So, what was Garner doing? Essentially resisting arrest. There were multiple officers pining him down, so it was arguable that the choke hold was excessive, but not a homicide. This is a case of possible police brutality, but there is no evidence of racism at all, and Whites too have been brutalised by police, more than Blacks in aggregate, as there are more Whites, and more White criminals.

https://www.nytimes.com/2014/12/04/nyregion/grand-jury-said-to-bring-no-charges-in-staten-island-chokehold-death-of-eric-garner.html

Interracial Homicide Offender and Victimization Rates by Race

With race war raging in America, you know, the Left claiming that every time a White person scratches themselves some act of racism occurs, it is worthwhile having a few stats to fling back. So, here they are:

https://www.unz.com/anepigone/interracial-homicide-offender-and-victimization-rates-by-race-us-2019/

In the previous post on interracial and intersexual homicide distributions in the US, Kratoklastes and Buzz Mohawk point out these distributions deal with absolute numbers, not rates. By rate, blacks are 11.4 times more likely to perpetrate interracial homicide than whites are, and others—a mishmash category including Asians, American Indians, and many people of mixed race—are 1.9 times more likely than whites to do so: Conversely, though, blacks are 2.5 times more likely than whites are to be the victims of interracial murder. Others are 1.2 times more likely to be so. Again, this concerns a small fraction, 15.7%, of all homicides in the US for which the race(s) of both victim and offender are known. The vast majority of homicide, 84.3%, occurs between members of the same race, broadly defined.

https://www.unz.com/sbpdl/his-name-is-tyler-wingate-24-year-old-white-man-gets-in-car-accident-with-black-male-in-83-black-detroit-black-motorist-beats-him-to-death/

Evil and Ugliness

In our culture, once upon a time, and to some degree the mythos still exists, goodness was associated with light, evil with darkness, something that must go back to our primal past. And, associated with this, is I think the recognition that evil people tend to be ugly. You can have a look at the villains at present on the US stage, you would not be wrong in taking most of them to be demons. A few days back a photo of one popular Left figure seemed to indicate growth deformities on her neck, leading to one wit writing that she was growing gills!

It was the philosopher Wittgenstein who said: "the human body is the best picture of the human soul." Being a philosopher, he was probably meaning to advance materialism, but there is another mytho-poetic reading of this claim. You can get a rough idea of what most people are like by looking at their faces. Physically beautiful people tend to be better quality people, not always, but at a statistically significant level.

https://www.insider.com/benefits-of-being-attractive-science-2018-12#companies-with-attractive-ceos-might-make-more-money-2

https://www.macleans.ca/society/science/the-mysterious-power-of-attractive-people/

https://www.psychologytoday.com/au/blog/games-primates-play/201203/the-truth-about-why-beautiful-people-are-more-successful

https://medium.com/swlh/attractive-people-are-more-likely-to-be-trusted-elected-and-listened-to-a0735869d2e8

As the Nordic/Northern European sub-race has produced many archetypes of human beauty, it is obvious that a movement based upon evil and ugliness would want to destroy them, to produce a world of uniform ugliness.

Nordicide

Georgie Anne Geyer, in her book, *Americans No More*, (Atlantic monthly press, (1996), wrote about Americans: "history is replete with the sagas of great defeats, of peoples wiped off the face of the earth, and of cultures transformed through clashes with others. Across and throughout history, nations fell, disintegrated, lost their nerve, made disastrous decisions, fought wars of self-destruction, and were not wise enough to sustain themselves. But I, at least, have never been able to discover another nation in human history, much less a great and powerful one, that literally willed itself out of existence through lethargy, and worst of all, guilt over things it did not even do."

This is well seen in the decline of the White population numbers as a proportion of the populations. The US, for example, is set to become non-White majority some think in about 10 years or so now; it was once estimated as 2050, then 2040. The whole of Western Europe, and even Australia is on track for the same fate at various times, but all well before 2050. Australia does not even keep track of its racial-ethnic profile. Demographer Charles Price used to publish work on this, but that was decades ago. One look at the Sydney CBD shows Australia's future as it slowly melts away.

What will happen? My guess is that things will not go so smoothly for the globalists, not because the pathetic

White sheeple will stage resistance, but because of the converging catastrophes discussed by Guillaume Faye (1949-2019).

https://books.google.com.au/books/about/Convergence_of_Catastrophes.html?id=pwg6J7KJIswC&redir_esc=y

https://books.google.com.au/books/about/Ethnic_Apocalypse.html?id=wDc5xwEACAAJ&redir_esc=y

In his book *Convergence of Catastrophes*, Faye predicted a collapse of global civilisation by 2020, which was a little too pessimistic. But, the trend is in place now. A collapse of the global system would generate forces that would work to counteract the present poisons killing the Nordic/Northern European people. The mind controlling rays could be turned off so that like out of some movie, our people could emerge from their present deracinated zombie state, and start being human again, instead of controlled mechanisms. There will be massively reduced numbers of everybody after the collapse, but sadly, that is how the cookie is going to crumble in the coming Darwinian world. Get ready.

White Racial Dispossession: Planned from the Beginning

The UN pushed on the policy of "non-discrimination" in the 1960s, it all coming together around 1965. The White Australia Policy look slightly longer to be murdered, but I have seen one MSM paper, dated 1945, when our boys were dying in the jungles of Asia, saying that the war indicates that the White Australia Policy will have to go, as if it caused the war. Ultimately all the politicians, Labor and Liberal, supported the abolition, or worked to undermine it. The link below is the official narrative, but once you read the American story below, you will be able to deconstruct its globalist Left narrative: https://www.nma.gov.au/defining-moments/resources/end-of-white-australia-policy

Here is what they did to America:

https://www.amren.com/news/2020/10/how-a-1965-immigration-law-forever-changed-the-makeup-of-america/

The Hart-Celler Immigration Amendments Act of 1965, enacted 55 years ago this week, struck down the race- and nationality-based quota law. When Lyndon B. Johnson signed the law, he modestly stated, "(T)his bill that we will sign today is not a revolutionary bill." Yet, the nation's foreign-born population rose from 9.6 million in 1965 to a record 44.8 million in 2018. According to the Pew Research Center, new immigrants, their children, and their grandchildren accounted for 55 percent of U.S. population growth from 1965 to 2015. The post-1965 act immigrants were much more diverse racially because immigrants arriving from Africa and Asia increased both in percentages and numbers. Immigrant admissions from the Americas increased in sheer numbers after 1965, particularly the Caribbean and Central America. In the years that followed, LBJ and the congressional sponsors of the legislation have been roundly criticized for understating how the repeal of the national origin quotas law would alter the racial and ethnic composition of the United States. The bill's supporters were not unimaginative or misguided. Rather, they minimized the bill because it did not accomplish all that they originally set out to do, particularly in the areas of high-skilled immigration and refugee admissions. The supporters, of course, knew it would create a more diverse flow of immigrants; ending racial discrimination that favored immigrants from Northern and Western Europe was the objective.

The supporters of the legislation also knew it would increase future flows, but they estimated that the increases would be modest — about 60,000 to 65,000 annually. Their calculations were based upon prior levels and existing backlogs. It was a "straight line" view of immigration that did not take into account other factors that might accelerate the flow, or other provisions in the legislation that might potentially alter future flows. This simplistic approach led to projections that overstated flows from some parts of the world and understated flows from other parts of the world. The legislation that became law on Oct. 3, 1965, was much more modest than earlier proposals. The law did not include the original emphasis on high-skilled immigration, nor did it provide for a system of refugee admissions. Advocates for immigration reform had to accept compromises in order to end the national origins system. It would be another 15 years before Congress passed the Refugee Act and 25 years before Congress expanded high-skilled immigration.

In short, while the date varies, in perhaps 10 or so years, America becomes majority non-White, and a Democrat dictatorship of Leftist policies. America collapses, if it does not after the Biden regime election, through civil war, one of the products of this cultural war. Even blind Freddy could have seen that this was the goal back then, but conservatives were too dumb or cowardly to see and fight it, their weakness on race being a fatal flaw. It still is with many still not seeing it, or not wanting to see it. How easy it is for conservatives to ignore inconvenient truths! Other examples could be given, by the bucket full.

The endgame of the liberal philosophy of non-discrimination is exactly the opposite, discrimination against Whites, as the policy immediately was highjacked and linked to the Great Replacement, and every other commo ideology from the insane 1960s. Thus, take Australia as an example, since we write about Canada every day. The White Australia Policy was soon replaced by multiculturalism, and then the Asianisation of Australia, which is nothing more than a Yellow Australia Policy, or non-White Australia Policy, certainly not something color-blind. Now the elites on the universities push the final agenda, of being part of China, the new super-power. In the past, no Asian country saw it necessary to change its racial profile and culture for trade, even when defeated in war, so that is the give-Thus, how could it be otherwise when the entire narrative is about replacing the old Anglo world, with the Asian one, as numerous academic stated in their articles and books; evidence fills many essays, but these are excellent summaries that I was referred to by my Aussie mates:

https://reduceimmigration.files.wordpress.com/2013/12/mccormack-d_the-grand-plan-asianisation-of-australia-race-place-and-power_1996.pdf

https://www.goodreads.com/book/show/20459271-new-britannia

Of course, it was not all done overnight, as McCormack and Allan James painstakingly document, but by the typical Fabian socialist strategy of gradualism, just as they did here in my native Canada, and down in the USA. Sounds like anti-White Leftist racism to me. Does anyone care? Certainly not the UN, who never stop wanting more of the same, until we are no more.

The Political Correctness of Philosophy

I have had a nodding interest in contemporary philosophy, which is full of all sorts of weird counter-common sense things, like minds don't exist, all that exists are the entities of physics, and you name it. All is up for grabs, to make name for young punks seeking jobs. But this has always been done within a politically correct framework, as this little story shows:

https://www.amren.com/news/2020/10/philosophy
-is-being-hijacked-by-woke-twitter-mobs/

> Philosophers tend to be highly influenced by their environment, and can often be found rationalizing instead of critically examining the conventional views of the people around them. But if anything warrants philosophical scrutiny, surely it is our national taboos. As a philosopher of biology, one taboo is of particular interest to me: the taboo on considering the possibility that genes play a role in group differences in psychological traits. So I wrote a paper arguing that, while nothing can be definitively proved, there is strongly suggestive evidence that genes are involved in group differences, and we should stop suppressing and censoring research into this topic.

> I submitted the paper to *Philosophical Psychology*—a respected journal that publishes work on the connection between philosophy and psychology, which at the time was co-edited by Mitchell Herschbach (a philosopher) and Cees van Leeuwen (a psychologist). To my pleasant surprise, I received two positive referee reports along with a request for revisions. After two rounds of review,

the paper was accepted and published in the January 2020 issue of the journal.

The paper was accompanied by an Editors' Note written by van Leeuwen and Herschbach, saying:

The decision to publish an article in *Philosophical Psychology* is based on criteria of philosophical and scientific merit, rather than ideological conformity... In sum, Cofnas' paper certainly adopts provocative positions on a host of issues related to race, genetics, and IQ. However, none of these positions are to be excluded from the current scientific and philosophical debates as long as they are backed up with logical argumentation and empirical evidence, and they deserve to be disputed rather than disparaged.

It didn't take long for the paper and Editors' Note to come to the attention of the wokerati on Twitter. Macquarie University philosophy professor Mark Alfano deemed my paper "shit" and announced his plan to "ruin [my] reputation permanently and deservedly." He started a petition on change.org demanding an "apology, retraction, or resignation (or some combination of these three)" from the journal editors. A number of philosophers—many of whom did not even read the paper—joined the campaign to get it retracted and/or smear me.

But the editors of *Philosophical Psychology* stood firm.

A group of six philosophers and three anthropologists—including Mark Alfano and City University of New York philosophy professor Massimo Pigliucci—submitted a comment on my paper to *Philosophical Psychology*, pedaling some familiar fallacies and strawmen.

Then they throw out the old canard that race can't be real because humans share 99.9 percent of their They don't mention that there are three billion base pairs in the human genome, and therefore *three million* base pairs where we are not identical, which could be the basis of race differences. {snip} In any case, crude comparisons of genetic similarity provide little information about the magnitude or significance of differences. We are 99.1 percent identical with chimpanzees in terms of functionally important DNA, but if that's all you told a space alien about the difference between us and chimps it would be pretty misleading.

Many prominent scientists have said openly that it is immoral to study this topic. Scholars who are seen as supporting hereditarianism are regularly fired from their jobs.

Then, out of the blue, van Leeuwen released a statement announcing his resignation:

> After 25 years at the journal, I am resigning as editor of *Philosophical Psychology*. The reason is the imminent publication of a commentary bypassing editor moderation. While my co-editor and part of the editorial board felt that a stream of insinuations and personal attacks on social media left them with no better choice, my resignation should be seen as taking a stand for an independent, non-partisan forum for philosophical debate.

> The remaining editor-in-chief, Mitchell Herschbach, who previously co-authored two separate statements defending the review process and the decision to publish my paper, published a grovelling apology.

Modern philosophy is a disgrace, and that is not even considering the stuff that shades into critical theory, feminism, queer studies, and the like. We would be better and healthier without this type of philosophy, and there would be an opportunity of re-establishing old school philosophy.

Do All Blue-Eyed Humans Have a Single Common Ancestor?

This story goes that once upon a time in a land, far, far away, everybody had brown eyes, but a genetic mutation affecting the OCA2 gene resulted in the creation of a "switch" on a gene adjacent to the OCA2 gene, reducing the production of P protein, and the level of melanin in the iris, making brown eyes blue, so to speak: H. Eiberg (et al.), "Blue Eye Color in Humans May be Caused by a Perfectly Associated Founder Mutation in a Regulatory Element Located within the HERC2 Gene Inhibiting OCA2 Expression," *Human Genetics*, vol. 123 (2), 2008: 177.

The argument is that the variation in eye colour from brown to green is due to the quantity of melanin in the iris. Allegedly, people with blue eyes have only a small variation in melanin levels. "From this we can conclude that all blue-eyed individuals are linked to the same ancestor. They have all inherited the same switch at exactly the same spot in their DNA," according to Eiberg.

As I see it, nothing as such flows about there being a single common ancestor as such, for all blue-eyed individuals. Who is to say that with the utter magic of mutations, the real engine of evolution (which natural selection selects), there could not have been a multi-regional origin of blue eyes? It is a fallacy of reason to infer from low variance to a single common ancestor.

Dark Ages Will be Really Dark (Like, No Lights On!)

There are an increasing number of essays on the internet, arguing against the popular trend in thought that the fall of Ancient Rome was not a catastrophe, but rather that the barbarian migrants integrated into Roman society, merely transforming it. Shit, does that view tell us something about the politics of today, or what! The most important book arguing against this happy face view of collapse is by Oxford don, Bryan Ward-Perkins, *The Fall of Rome and the End of Civilization* (Oxford University press, 2006). Assembled there is a wealth of evidence showing that the standard of living in Rome after the fall, was that of prehistoric times. It was cultural and technological catastrophe, involving a great die off of thousands.

https://www.amazon.com/Fall-Rome-End-Civilization/dp/0192807285

https://www.bu.edu/historic/hs/perkins.pdf

https://www.youtube.com/watch?v=erHrL7UV27Y

Thus, dark ages were really dark. This is important for us, because there is a strong case that the West is the modern Rome, and that we are heading into the same horrors, indeed, greater horrors, that will sink us. Almost all of the factors that brought Rome down, are here, right now.

https://www.theoccidentalobserver.net/2020/02/01/the-new-dark-ages-in-western-europe-and-north-america-comparisons-with-the-fall-of-rome/

Against Against Accelerationism

Greg Johnson, at Counter-Curents.com, explains the doctrine of accelerationism as follows: "Accelerationism is the idea that the best way to achieve White Nationalist goals is to accelerate the decline of the present system. This will supposedly have two effects. First, acceleration will weaken the system's ability to maintain power, including to oppress dissenters. Second, acceleration will anger and awaken the white masses, making them more receptive to our message."

https://www.counter-currents.com/2020/01/against-accelerationism/

Once we accept that the system is occupied, not by our kind, that the rulers are unelected Deep Staters and other elites, and that we deplorables are ear-marked for the Great Replacement, the conservativism of the past, and past strategies and tactics, need drastic modification. Accelerationism, or as others have called it, "destructionism," looks forward to the collapse of the system as needed for any chance of rebuilding, since reform of what exists now is simply impossible. Look at Trump as the last chance of any sort of mainstream political answer to the problems that confront us.

Johnson makes the following point against accelerationism: "When black rule came to South Africa and Rhodesia, the cascading disasters did not galvanize white self-assertion but instead led to an almost complete collapse of white morale and resistance. ...Worse (for them) is not necessarily better (for us). Worse is sometimes just worse. So, praying for bad news—or actively promoting bad outcomes—seems like a very foolish way to create a better world. In fact, it seems akin to suicide bombing: an act of a people reduced to hopelessness and desperation after a long train of defeats. ...No, actually we lose by losing. When we lose, we can of course hope that somehow the gods or will turn our defeats into conditions for future victories. But in the end, we can only win by winning."

This is still thinking within the paradigm that the system will continue, that there will be clearly defined winners and losers, and that the system will not suffer from collapse threats, as described by numerous sources:

https://www.amazon.com/Survive-Economic-Collapse-Piero-Giorgio/dp/1593680147

There is thus a major epistemological difference between one wanting old commo Bernie to beat Trump, which will merely replicate the South African oppressive situation and demoralise whites, and instead hoping for the entire Temple of Evil of modernity to crumble from globally destructive events, such as pandemics, a new Carrington EMP Event, and global economic collapse. Hell, even an asteroid strike would be helpful to turn of the mind control mechanisms of modernity and return man to a naturalistic understanding of reality, instead of our present Leftist, force-fed social constructionism, where men have no more real freedom than force-fed battery hens.

The dark cloud of civilizational collapse does have a silver lining. Here is another point of view, one which looks beyond the present paradigm that most nationalists of any color live in, after the state and all its discontents, crumbles and falls:

http://www.returnofkings.com/88671/4reasonswhyc ollapsewillbethebestthingtohappenformen

The collapse will mean the restoration of natural order: the rule of the jungle. In fact, I think it would be wrong to call the destruction of our so-called civilization as a "collapse"; it would simply be a return to the way things were. No more corporate serfdom, no more putrid consumerism, no more technological slavery, and no safe spaces for the cry-babies to hide and cry in. Wimps, complainers, and the weak will not survive. People will once again be naturally selected instead of being artificially sheltered.

One of the best aspect of the new order would be the return of masculine virtue. As I've said, any new society that people form must be defended against external threats. This is not an option. And only an organized group of men with strength, courage, mastery, and honor (as per Jack Donovan) will prevail in the post-apocalyptic world. Men will be men again.

Who knows what savage energy is begging to be unleashed within that man serving as an office drone? Who knows if that guy flipping burgers for a minimum wage will become the future tribal leader? How many men today are living jaded and unfulfilling lives when they could be fighters and warriors instead?

Can't wait until men are allowed to be men again? Then you better be ready for the war for survival.

And guess what? There won't be feminist harpies demanding "equality" when strong men are needed to rebuild civilization and defend against gangs and rival tribes. They'll be begging for some of that "toxic" masculinity to come and protect them. They'll kneel in submission to a patriarchal order faster than they would have screamed "rape!" in the previous world. Suddenly, with their government boyfriend gone and the internet white knights nowhere to be found, their whole feminist charade will shatter and the ridiculousness of it all will become apparent. The unstable and fat ones will likely disappear first as they offer no value to anyone.

Also in the new world, the SJWs and the rest of the progressive freaks will die faster than a gay snowman in Saudi Arabia. No more bitching and insulting each other on the internet, no more trying to censor or ruin other people, and no more crying for sympathy and victim privileges. There won't be anymore idiotic debates about who is right or wrong: only who survives and who doesn't. The struggle for life without civilization will be face to face and man to man. I would love to see how well the loser male-feminists fare against the very men they love to bash without a computer screen to hide behind.

The future without the gynocentric system is a future where men will dominate.

The longing in many men, perhaps found in the playing of apocalyptic video games, in TV shows about the zombie apocalypse, and other post-system material, is a longing for a return of a world where strength, honour and heroism is valued. If accelerationism, brings this on, then bring it on, quickly! In fact, I hope acceleration accelerates, you know, d^3v/ds^3.

Will Islam Conquer the World? Intelligence and IQ Makes No Difference

A new book by the highly productive Edward Dutton, *Why Islam Makes You Stupid ... but Also Means You'll Conquer the World* (2020), is actually a solid, implicit critique of IQ fetishism of sites like *American Renaissance* which has, in my opinion, an excessive, obsessive conception of the relevance of IQ, based upon contestable studies, as all of psychology is. Dutton takes a longer evolutionary view, which sees ethnocentrism and reproductive success as ultimately deciding the destiny of the world. A sister publication, Vdare.com, has a review, as we are all too poor to buy books here, we quote the essence:

https://vdare.com/articles/will-islam-will-prove-that-demographics-is-destiny

> Though rigorous adherence to Islam suppresses intelligence, the advantages conferred by ethnocentrism and fertility are so great that, in the everlasting conflict between the Islam and formerly-Christian Europe, the former will triumph despite the intellectual and technological advantages of the latter.

> Dutton, in his usual resolute and confident style, packs his exploration of Islam with information and original insights to reveal how the religion affects the IQ not only of Muslims but also the Europeans whose lands Mohammed's disciples are colonizing.

> Chapter 1 introduces modern research on intelligence in the context of human biodiversity and

group selection: You pass on your genes by having children, by investing in your kind, or by investing in your group.

Chapter 6 closes the book with Dutton's reflections of Western man's future in light of the general deterioration of Western civilizational strength, the declining average intelligence of Europeans, and the accelerating immigration into the European heartlands of aliens in general and Muslims in particular.

But Dutton, originally educated as a theologian, is at his strongest in the middle when dealing with Islam's stultifying effects on IQ—which will not, he predicts, thwart its triumph over the West. ...

In Chapter 2, Dutton summarizes the interplay between intelligence and religiosity. Overall, there exists a weak negative correlation between IQ and religiosity, and the harsher and more fundamentalist the creed, the lower the average IQ of its adepts.

That might seem trivial, as professors of science or engineers are rarely ardent believers, but two existential threats arise from the association of IQ and religiousness and their effect on fertility. A positive correlation between religiousness and fertility is dysgenic in terms of IQ; i.e.,

- more intelligent but less religious people have fewer children;
- less intelligent and more religious people have more children.

Dutton describes at length the negative consequences for the economy and technological development of Islam. But the real import of that fact: More religious and less intelligent neighboring nations will achieve a demographic advantage over more intelligent states."

I agree that the West is in fact demographically doomed, in the longer term, and all civilisations collapse. Ironically, those who champion IQ and technological sophistication, who either have no children, putting egg-headed pursuits first, or have below the replacement level, will ultimately have their high IQ genes disappear from the world. How smart was that? Evolution and natural selection laugh last.

There Goes England!
Deracination Unlimited!

If we can still believe surveys, 90 percent of England believes that being English is not about colour, yes, 90 percent, supposedly:

https://www.theguardian.com/society/2019/jun/30/being-english-not-about-colour-say-majority

The number of people who believe that in order to be English you have to be white has halved over the past seven years, with the older generation apparently driving a wider acceptance of people with different ethnic backgrounds.

Just over 10% of people believe that ethnicity is an important determining factor in being English, compared to 20% from a 2012 study, according to British Future and the Centre for English Identity and Politics, which is about to publish its follow-up to the 2012 study, *This Sceptred Isle*.

The biggest change was noted among over-65s, where the importance of whiteness fell from 35% to 16%. The new data could challenge the perception that the 2016 Brexit referendum reflected an increase in xenophobic English identity. The findings suggest that during the time of the Brexit vote, perceptions of English identity were becoming more, rather than less, ethnically inclusive.

A contributing factor to this shift in perceptions is likely to be emergence of examples of English diversity. Gareth Southgate's squad for the 2018 World Cup in

Russia was a prominent example. Southgate described the England squad as a team that represented "modern England". In an ITV interview, he said: "We've spent a bit of time being lost as to what our modern identity is, and I think as a team we represent that modern identity and hopefully people can connect with us."

This was echoed by Sunder Katwala, director of British Future. "An inclusive England may be symbolised by Raheem Sterling and Nikita Parris scoring goals for England, or Moeen Ali taking wickets in the World Cup, but it also reflects the lived reality of who most of us now think of as English."

Other signifiers of English identity saw a smaller change. Previous results showed 56% of participants thought it was important for your parents to have been born in England, and the latest show 48% do – marking a drop of 8%. "There has been an important generational shift in how we think about England and the English," said Katwala. "There has been no doubt that most people who have migrated to England, like my parents, usually felt they were invited to become British but not often to identify as English, too. An increasing number of their children, born in England, have felt they can choose to identify as English as well as British."

However, the survey showed that three factors – being born in England, paying taxes in England and contributing to English society – were seen as important in being English by more than 70% of the population.

Similar polling carried out by YouGov in 2018 revealed that members of BAME communities are still significantly less likely to consider themselves English. However, the perception that being English is strongly related to being born in England could allow new generations of BAME citizens to be more readily acknowledged as English.

John Denham, director of the Centre for English Identity and Politics, said: "The idea that English is an ethnic identity is widely repeated in the media and politics. That Englishness has become even more inclusive at a time in which our society has become more divided is to be welcomed.

"Ethnicity is clearly much less important outside a small hardcore of residents. The further development of an inclusive Englishness would benefit from positive engagement by leaders across the political spectrum. This should aim to encourage BAME citizens to see English identity as open to them and that the strongest English identifiers continue to support the opening up of English identity."

It is hard to say what to make of this, given the diminishing number of whites in England, with major cities like London becoming majority non-white, and mass immigration has changed the very nature of England, making the concept of England essentially meaningless anyway.

https://www.breitbart.com/europe/2019/05/25/600 000-migrants-arrive-in-uk-in-one-year/

In this context though it is interesting to speculate how the deracinated English whites would feel about the Dalai Lama's claim that Europe, and of course the UK, will become Muslim if migrants are allowed to stay:

https://www.amren.com/news/2019/06/dalai-lama-europe-will-become-muslim-if-migrants-allowed-to-stay/

https://www.breitbart.com/europe/2019/06/27/dalai -lama-europe-will-become-muslim-if-migrants-allowed-to-stay/?fbclid=IwAR0nAC2Lk1pYml68iEyjr-NnO7nskGPdwVHqlEhGeXI9NVnzQ52oJrx_MrQ

The Dalai Lama insisted Wednesday that "Europe is for Europeans," warning that if too many migrants are allowed to stay, the continent could become "Muslim" or "African."

The Buddhist spiritual leader, who has been living as a refugee in India since fleeing Tibet in 1959, told the BBC that only a "limited number" of migrants should be permitted to reside in Europe.

The 83-year-old said Europe should take in refugees and offer them an education, but then send them back to their homelands.

"European countries should take these refugees and give them education and training, then the aim is return to their own land," he said.

The BBC host asked what should happen if migrants want to stay in their adopted countries, to which the Dalai Lama replied:

"A limited number is OK, but whole Europe eventually become Muslim country? Impossible. Or African country? Also impossible."

Asked what was wrong with the scenario of Europe becoming Muslim or African, he said: "They themselves I think better to their own land. Keep Europe for Europeans."

This was not the first time the Tibetan leader has voiced these opinions. In a speech last year in Malmo, Sweden, the Dalai Lama reiterated that migrants should not stay in Europe but should return to help rebuild their own countries.

"Receive them, help them, educate them, but ultimately they should develop their own country," he said at the time. "I think Europe belongs to the Europeans."

Now the deracinate 90 percenters should be happy having say, a 90 percent Muslim society, with sharia law. And, they could call it "England" too! But if so, that seems inconsistent with other actions indicating some extreme nervousness about fast approaching minority status, indicating that they may well be telling interview people what they want to hear, while still having a secret fear of diversity replacement:

https://www.independent.co.uk/news/education/education-news/parents-religious-education-islam-headteachers-liverpool-hope-university-study-a8976366.html

https://www.dailymail.co.uk/news/article-7204663/Afghan-asylum-seeker-fuelled-desire-kill-English-people.html

https://www.rt.com/news/463033-denmark-school-indoctrination-integration/

https://www.dailymail.co.uk/news/article-7190711/Parents-pulling-pupils-dont-want-children-visit-mosques.html

https://www.breitbart.com/europe/2019/06/28/khans-london-thefts-subway-surge-80-per-cent-three-years/

https://voiceofeurope.com/2019/06/over-90-percent-of-swedes-think-islam-is-incompatible-with-human-rights/

https://www.amren.com/commentary/2019/06/the-african-population-bomb/

https://www.brookings.edu/research/less-than-half-of-us-children-under-15-are-white-census-shows/

https://www.dailymail.co.uk/news/article-7196313/The-slow-death-English-village-Author-ROBIN-PAGE-decline-Cambridgeshire-idyll.html

https://www.theguardian.com/society/2019/jul/17/renting-millennials-homelessness-crisis-retire

Still, it would not surprise me if the white English were happy with their dissolution, given the present state of ethno-cultural decadence and degeneracy. It did not take long for a super power to become, well, nothing much, really.

The Age of the European Race:
The Extinction of Genetic Diversity

Here is one reason why the great replacement of the European peoples should be resisted: they have made an irreplaceable contribution to human history, and are not a flash in the pan as some conservative sites which are supposed to defend the white ethno-racial group think, but are an ancient contribution to the human species:

https://phys.org/news/2019-07-oldest-africa-reset-human-migration.html

"A 210,000-year-old skull has been identified as the earliest modern human remains found outside Africa, putting the clock back on mankind's arrival in Europe by more than 150,000 years, researchers said Wednesday.

In a startling discovery that changes our understanding of how modern man populated Eurasia, the findings support the idea that Homo sapiens made several, sometimes unsuccessful migrations from Africa over tens of thousands of years.

Southeast Europe has long been considered a major transport corridor for modern humans from Africa. But until now the earliest evidence of Homo sapiens on the continent dated back only around 50,000 years.

There has however been a number of discoveries indicating the ancient presence of Neanderthals—an early human cousin—across the continent.

Two fossilised but badly damaged skulls unearthed in a Greek cave in the 1970s were identified as Neanderthal at the time.

In findings presented in the journal *Nature*, an international team of researchers used state-of-the art computer modelling and uranium dating to re-examine the two skulls.

One of them, named Apidima 2 after the cave in which the pair were found, proved to be 170,000 years old and did indeed belong to a Neanderthal.

But, to the shock of scientists, the skull named Apidima 1 pre-dated Apidima 2 by as much as 40,000 years, and was determined to be that of a Homo sapiens.

That makes the skull by far the oldest modern human remains ever discovered on the continent, and older than any known Homo sapiens specimen outside of Africa.

"It shows that the early dispersal of Homo sapiens out of Africa not only occurred earlier, before 200,000 years ago, but also reached further geographically, all the way to Europe," Katerina Harvati, a palaeoanthropologist at the Eberhard Karls University of Tuebingen, Germany, told AFP."

https://www.theatlantic.com/science/archive/2019/07/apidima-greek-skull-oldest-human-fossil-outside-africa/593563/

That all assumes the Out of Africa hypothesis, but there are cracks developing in that politically correct ideology, as detailed here:

https://www.telegraph.co.uk/science/2017/05/22/europe-birthplace-mankind-not-africa-scientists-find/

"The history of human evolution has been rewritten after scientists discovered that Europe was the birthplace of mankind, not Africa.

Currently, most experts believe that our human lineage split from apes around seven million years ago in central Africa, where hominids remained for the next five million years before venturing further afield.

But two fossils of an ape-like creature which had human-like teeth have been found in Bulgaria and Greece, dating to 7.2 million years ago.

The discovery of the creature, named Graecopithecus freybergi, and nicknameded 'El Graeco' by scientists, proves our ancestors were already starting to evolve in Europe 200,000 years before the earliest African hominid.

An international team of researchers say the findings entirely change the beginning of human history and place the last common ancestor of both chimpanzees and humans - the so-called Missing Link - in the Mediterranean region.

t that time climate change had turned Eastern Europe into an open savannah which forced apes to find new food sources, sparking a shift towards bipedalism, the researchers believe.

"This study changes the ideas related to the knowledge about the time and the place of the first steps of the humankind," said Professor Nikolai Spassov from the Bulgarian Academy of Sciences.

"Graecopithecus is not an ape. He is a member of the tribe of hominins and the direct ancestor of homo.

"The food of the Graecopithecus was related to the rather dry and hard savannah vegetation, unlike that of the recent great apes which are living in forests. Therefore, like humans, he has wide molars and thick enamel."

The European racial heritage is something worth preserving, and for those racial nihilists who think that it is not, let's not preserve any animal species either. Take them all down, and die on a barren desert of a planet, which seems to be the goal of the globalists who want a burnt-out planet to encircle the sun until it is destroyed by that sun's own death. So much for

Is White Genocide a "Myth"?

The Affirmative Right web site, not to be confused with affirmative action, publishes some great material, and some not so great, and some deserving solid critique. The article discussed here maintains that Whites are largely responsible for their plight, and as hard as is to accept, some good points are made:

https://affirmativeright.blogspot.com/2019/12/the-myth-of-white-genocide.html

> The truth is that white men are primarily responsible for the destruction of the West. White men liberated women from their traditional role as housewife and mother. Nowadays, women are encouraged to spend their prime reproductive years getting an education and pursuing a career. The consequences of this unrestrained female hypergamy are a lower white fertility rate and the destruction of the traditional monogamous family unit. In 1919, the US Congress ratified the 19th Amendment, giving females the right to vote. Concerning this regressive legislation, academics write:

> "Suffrage coincided with immediate increases in state government expenditures and revenue and more liberal voting patterns for federal representatives, and these effects continued growing over time as more women took advantage of the franchise" (Lott and Kenny, 1999).

> Whites ensured passage of the 1964 Civil Rights Act, ending racial segregation in the southern states. If it wasn't for the civil rights movement, blacks would have

remained segregated and the black-on-white crime rate would be insignificant.

The 1965 Immigration Act, which inaugurated America's demographic transformation, only became law because of white power and influence. The US is now on a direct path to becoming a North American version of Brazil by the middle of the 21st century. If not for whites, there wouldn't be a feminist or a civil rights movement ... white problems are caused by millions of gullible ... white voters and their globalist elites.

Some, especially in the Alt-Right as it now exists, believe the Western democracies are somehow preventing the white majority from organizing *en masse* to resist their own racial "displacement," but this is a laughable excuse.

Firstly, given the demographic emergency, why are white nationalists still such a very small percentage of the population of North America and Western Europe? That few whites actively sympathize with white nationalist causes is empirically supported by numerous surveys and questionnaires. For example, in the US, the Institute of Government and Public Affairs has published data showing that white majority opposition to school integration and interracial marriage, once common during the 1940s and 1950s, has largely evaporated. An ANES survey (2016) reports that only 6 percent of white respondents expressed support for white identity politics.

Secondly, if whites were as naturally pro-white as some people claim they are, they would have long ago voted white activists into office to put an end to the Cultural Revolution of the 1960s. We would have been treated to an unbroken succession of white nationalist governments. There would have been a President David Duke and a Prime Minister Nick Griffin. Instead, whites show their disdain for pro-white advocacy by voting for the same neoliberal globalist parties *ad nauseam*. Pierre

Trudeau, the architect of the modern liberal police state in Canada, was voted into office four times, despite allowing non-whites to enter the country and become "new Canadians" during his first term as prime minister.

That is correct, whatever area you care to look, the general apathy, ignorance, cowardice and suicidal nature of "we, the people" can be seen. Thus, 90 percent of the English believe that having a white ethnic link to the country, even though this link of blood goes back thousands of years, is not necessary to be English, especially if one is a football star.

The conclusion that follows is... "White nationalists believe that non-white immigration is "white genocide," but is this an accurate perception of reality? What would we be seeing if demographic genocide was really occurring in Western countries? What do we see in Tibet and Xinjiang, where there is indisputable evidence of demographic genocide? We see a long record of wars, rebellions, terrorist attacks, and widespread civil unrest in response to state-enforced migratory policies, which continue despite the overwhelming numerical and military superiority of the Chinese occupation.

When it comes to whites, we see no resistance of any kind. Whites neither wage wars, rebel, or commit terrorist acts against their supposedly "oppressive" Western governments, even though they have both the numbers and technical ability to do so if they wanted to.

Why the inertia?

The answer is that whites want to be demographically replaced; they do not want to be saved, least of all by other, more level-headed whites. The demographic transformation of the West is occurring because of mass democracy, not because of the "soft" totalitarian policies of the globalist elite. These are a consequence, not a cause, of the demographic transformation of the West.

Notwithstanding Bob Whitaker's online mantra, "white genocide" is a myth. By calling white race replacement "genocide," we trivialize the enormity of this crime for cheap rhetorical purposes. Not only is non-white immigration not "white genocide," it isn't "invasion" either, since non-whites have been invited by whites to settle in white countries. Neither are whites being ethnically cleansed or "dispossessed" of their own nations, since they are freely giving away everything they have received from their ancestors, often with smiles on their faces.

In this case, non-white replacement migration is more accurately described as collective white racial suicide, which is not the same thing as genocide, invasion, and ethnic cleansing.

... There will be no collective white racial awakening. The diversity madness will not end until the West is utterly destroyed. As it now stands, a solution to this pitiable state of affairs remains an elusive one. Peaceful dissemination of race realist and white nationalist ideas seldom accomplishes anything. Whites, many of whom are already familiar with the biological reality of race and sex, will continue to uphold the neoliberal order, regardless of what the latest science says (just like Richard Nixon and Ronald Reagan did).

Thus, what we are seeing is white racial suicide, aided of course by the powerful elites, so it is an assisted suicide, very assisted. The ordinary people are the fuel, and the elites the spark, that burns down the West. But, all the author can say in conclusion as a response to all of this poison, is that there needs to be separation from the mainstream, but does not detail how this would be done, and what the point is, although I do agree.

One way that has been suggested, is accelerationism, the idea that the decline, and collapse of the present system may awaken our people, and kick into being a survival mechanism, like the hypnotic power being turned off. Greg Johnson rejects this position of accelerationism:

https://www.counter-currents.com/2020/01/against-accelerationism/#more-114734

"No, actually we lose by losing. When we lose, we can of course hope that somehow the gods or "history" will turn our defeats into conditions for future victories. But in the end, we can only win by winning."

That is all well and good, but the issue is that things may be so far gone, so contaminated, the field so overgrown with metaphorical choking toxic weeds, that it is no longer possible to try and save things, or clear the land, problem by problem. Systems collapse, falling apart from its own internal rottenness, may be the final hope. It will destroy the tyranny and give us the opportunity to rebuild, or at least die out with dignity.

White Eliminationism: An Establishment Philosophy Now

The medical journal, *The Lancet*, has become lefty political of late, not just with climate change, but with racial identity issues. For example, the latest controversy involves a review of Jonathan Metzl's *Dying of Whiteness: How the Politics of Racial Resentment is Killing America's Heartland*, (Basic Books, New York, 2019), by Rhea Boyd: "Despair Doesn't Kill, Defending Whiteness Does" (January 11, 2020).

First, Metzl takes the predictable line that America's refusal to ban guns lies with white supremacy, and defending the racial hierarchy. Gun control is a symbolic issue reflecting white privilege, even though most gun deaths are of Whites, who "die for a cause." This is a crazy thesis that is refuted by the work on the gun issue by John Lott and many others, including Jews for the Preservation of Firearms Ownership, that has resources to debunk every assertion made by Metzl against private firearm ownership. He should consider debating them:

https://en.wikipedia.org/wiki/John_Lott

http://jpfo.org/

However, the issue now is with Rhea Boyd, who said on Twitter that whiteness needs to be eliminated, but she deleted the tweet when the storm blew in:

"I'm about to say something you might not be ready to hear.

But I'm going to say it anyways.

Despair isn't killing white Americans. The armed defense of structural whiteness is.

The solution?

Eliminate whiteness all together.

Thread.

— Rhea Boyd, MD (@RheaBoydMD) January 10, 2020

Yes, that is MD, a doctor.

https://www.breitbart.com/the-media/2020/01/12/lancet-only-way-stop-racism-eliminate-whiteness-all-together/

Then there is *The Lancet* review, which Breitbart has nicely summarised, with all the disgusting, inflammatory parts:

> In his book, Metzl argues that white mortality is up in the United States ever since the 2016 election of Donald Trump, since in order to "maintain an imagined place atop a racial hierarchy," white Americans who harbor "racial resentment" support policies that seem to limit the freedoms or resources available to non-whites, even though such decisions threaten their own wellbeing as well.
>
> "From expansive gun legislation to broad divestment in government programmes, Metzl characterises white liberties that endanger white lives or imperil white futures as 'dying of whiteness,'" Boyd observes.
>
> While in her review Boyd fundamentally agrees with Metzl's contentions, she believes that he is too soft on whites by attributing whites' self-destructive white

political actions to "racial resentment," which "erases white agency through emotional euphemism."

"At times, Metzl artfully articulates and historicises the racist origins of white interest in firearm fanaticism and 'small government' politics," Boyd writes. "At others, he turns to 'racial anxieties,' racially charged 'fears,' or 'racial resentment' to describe white people's political investment in white racial dominance."

Boyd decries the "common practice" of mis-attributing "white self-destruction and violence to psychological states" or obscuring "the impacts of defending whiteness through emotional euphemisms."

Drivers of white mortality such as suicide, chronic liver disease, and drug and alcohol poisoning have been described as "diseases of despair," Boyd notes, while they should be classified as "diseases of disproportionate opportunity (to wield firearms) and access (to prescription opiates)."

The real focus should not be on "mental illness," "distress," or "white fragility" underlying increasing white mortality, she contends, but rather on the fundamental "legacy of death in whiteness's wake."

It is a mistake — she asserts — to "assert that resentment, despair, or any emotion that arises from being 'left behind' accounts for white Americans' self-destructive actions, violent politics, or declining population health."

The real population that has been left behind are blacks, she argues, but the difference is that blacks have consistently supported policies that benefit everyone while whites only support policies that benefit themselves.

And so, "despite suffering at every turn of every decade of every century in this nation, generations of Black Americans have sought political reforms that expand electoral participation, increase government protections, and extend public resources beyond their individual or group benefit," she claims.

Thus, even from white suffering, Black victimisation flows. But, wait, there is more:

"Therefore, "scholars, the media, and the public" have failed to understand "the evolving ways white Americans continue to mobilise to maintain or extend the exclusive advantages whiteness offers those who can become white, even as those advantages place them in increasing proximity to death."

The simple fact is that "despair isn't killing white America, the armed defence of whiteness is," she writes. Thus, death "is the inevitable consequence of the full realisation of structural racism and the exclusive rights and resources it offers those who can become white," she continues.

Boyd goes on to propose a theory would challenge even the most race-obsessed, in part because it lacks any kind of rational intelligibility.

"For humans to use whiteness to manufacture access and privilege," Boyd suggests, "they must engineer scarcity and loss. This entanglement between access and scarcity, privilege and loss, means white people's unearned advantages have always been tethered to a legacy of untold deaths."

Despite his noble efforts to understand the evils of structural white racism, Boyd suggests, Metzl fails because he anchors it to an emotional foundation, which leads him to conclude that more healthy and self-reflective frameworks of structural whiteness are needed.

In reality, Boyd concludes, the only real solution "is to eliminate whiteness all together."

The fact that some people think this way is frightening enough. That the *Lancet*, which once represented serious medical journalism, would decide to publish it points to a devastating deterioration of the institutional academy as reasoned discourse gives way to incoherent ranting."

https://www.thelancet.com/journals/lancet/article/PIIS0140-6736(19)33147-2/fulltext

There have already been systematic demolitions of Boyd, notably by Steve Sailer at Unz.com.

https://www.unz.com/isteve/lancet-despair-doesnt-kill-defending-whiteness-does/

And, of course, there is the rejoinder, that Black on White crime dwarfs, proportionate to the populations, White on Black crime, and that even the MSM sometimes say that the main killers of African Americans, are other African Americans:

https://www.nationalreview.com/magazine/2019/12/22/the-need-to-discuss-black-on-black-crime/

https://www.amren.com/the-color-of-crime/

https://nypost.com/2017/09/26/all-that-kneeling-ignores-the-real-cause-of-soaring-black-homicides/

The FBI released its official crime tally for 2016 on Monday, and the data flies in the face of the rhetoric that professional athletes rehearsed in revived Black Lives Matter protests over the weekend.

Nearly 900 additional blacks were killed in 2016 compared with 2015, bringing the black homicide victim total to 7,881. Those 7,881 "black bodies," in the parlance of Ta-Nehisi Coates, are 1,305 more than the number of white victims (which in this case includes most Hispanics) for the same period, though blacks are only 13 percent of the nation's population.

The increase in black homicides last year comes on top of a previous 900-victim increase between 2014 and 2015.

Who is killing these black victims? Not whites, and not the police, but other blacks.

The same is said in an article sitting behind a paywall, The Washington Post.com, October 24, 2017, "America's Big Issue is 'Black Africans' Killing Each other." No discussion of this from people like Boyd.

But, what does eliminating whiteness mean? It cannot just be the elimination of white privilege, because no matter what Whites do, they have this like original sin. Thus, the thesis must be one of racial genocide, that eliminating whiteness is code word for eliminating Whites, for whiteness is just a property of white particulars. Maybe that is why American Whites want their guns. After all, just imagine talk about eliminating some other colored people; that would be genocide. So, what is good for the goose, is good for the gander.

https://www.naturalnews.com/2019-12-13-truths-that-we-the-people-have-spontaneously-come-to-realize.html

https://www.zerohedge.com/political/10-self-evident-truths-we-people-have-spontaneously-come-realize

Ethnic Apocalypse by Guillaume Faye

The late Guillaume Faye, French dissent right intellectual has had his final book released: *Ethnic Apocalypse: The Coming European Civil War* (Arktos, London, 2019). The French title actually translates as *A Racial Civil War*, but the English publisher did not run with that, worried that the book would get banned or whatever. Pathetic.

I will not give a blow by blow account of the book because it essentially follows topics that have been well discussed here, including changing demographics making white Europeans minorities in their own land, and festering crime. Here is some more recent material that this book on the same theme:

https://www.theoccidentalobserver.net/2019/09/08/a-race-war-prophecy/

https://voiceofeurope.com/2019/09/german-citizens-are-arming-themselves-with-firearms/

https://www.jihadwatch.org/2019/08/germany-25-of-the-population-and-42-of-young-children-now-of-migrant-backgrounds

https://www.amren.com/commentary/2019/08/the-color-of-knife-crime-in-britain/

https://voiceofeurope.com/2019/07/migrant-child-gang-puts-fear-into-neighbours-swedish-children-scared-to-go-outside/

https://www.amren.com/news/2019/07/the-majority-population-in-german-cities-is-facing-its-end/

"Frankfurt am Main, Offenbach, Heilbronn, Sindelfingen — in these and other cities, Germans with no immigration background are still the largest group, but are no longer an absolute majority. That affects West Germany more than the East, and cities more than non-urban areas.

As early as the 1980s, the Greens were propagating Multiculti — a multicultural society. Although it had already begun some time before, the very thought of it was hair-raising for some voters. This reality has been accentuated in recent decades. Although the phrase is somewhat out of style. Nowadays, we talk of diversity and mixed society. Meanwhile, the majority society is approaching its end in German cities. That means that Germans who have no immigration background (as defined by the Federal Office of Statistics) are no longer the statistical majority (>50%), but are just the largest of three groups, with foreigners and Germans with an immigration background.

Frankfurt is the Vanguard

The majority society has already ceased to exist in Frankfurt am Main. This is also true for some smaller cities like Offenbach (only 37% still native German), Heilbronn, Sindelfingen and Pforzheim, explains the immigration expert Jens Schneider, who does research at the University of Osnabrück. The same thing will happen soon in several other German cities. In early 2018, according to the city's statistical yearbook, 46.9% were native Germans. Germans with immigration background were 23.6% and foreigners — 53.1% together. The proportion of native Germans has declined in recent decades. The 50% threshold was first crossed in 2015 with 48.8%. Schneider rejects putting

Germans with immigration background and foreigners in the same pot, and, like many of his colleagues, advocates revising the categories. The concept of immigration background gives a false impression. In fact, ca. two thirds of all children of Germans with immigration background (including children of foreigners) are born in Germany. They are therefore German and would often have the prospect of a much better professional career than their parents.

There Is No More Majority Society

By present reckoning, Frankfurt a.M. is probably the only major city where the majority society has flipped, with Germans with an immigration background and foreigners at 53.1%. According to the "Intercultural Integration Report of 2017" of the city of Munich, Nuremberg (44.6%), Stuttgart (44.1%), Munich (43.2%) and Düsseldorf (40.2%) also show high percentages of foreigners and Germans with immigration background.

Strong Economy Attracts Immigrants

In Stuttgart, that percentage is now 46%. According to the press office of the capital city of Baden-Württemberg, almost 60% of under-18 residents of Stuttgart have an immigration background (including foreigners). The entire relationship will change in coming years, so that there will no longer be an ethnically defined majority. This is already the case in other communities.

It is almost exclusively West German and some South German cities that are affected. This may be because of the economic power of the South and the related need for labor. At any rate, there are also a number of cities where the proportion of these groups is considerably less. They tend to be in the East and North of Germany. In Hannover and Berlin, for instance, it is only ca. 30%, in Kiel 24%, in Potsdam 12%

and in Dresden 11% (figures from end of 2016). Before unification, the East German states had very little immigration, and this is reflected in today's numbers.

According to the Federal Statistical Office a person has immigration background if that person or at least one parent was not born a German citizen. The definition comprises the following individuals: 1) foreigners whether immigrants or not; 2) naturalized citizens, whether immigrants or not; 3) (recent) ethnic re-settlers; and 4) progeny of the first three groups born with German citizenship. There are slightly different definitions in some federal states.

If we look at the entire area of the Federal Republic, Germany in 2017 had 81.7 million residents, among them 62.5 million Germans without an immigration background (76.5%). Nationally, Germans without immigration background will remain an absolute majority for the foreseeable future. Germans with immigration background will reach 12.5% (9.8 million) of the entire population, and foreigners 11.9% (9.4 million). Here too, the declining proportional trend of Germans without immigration background could continue. Among children from 0 to 10 years old, the proportion of Germans without immigration background is easily 60%; among 10 to 15-year-olds, 64%.

https://www.investmentwatchblog.com/demographic-suicide-of-europe/

Will there be a civil war? That is the big question. The evidence indicates that the social capital necessary to maintain the level of civilisation the West once knew is rapidly draining away, so there is not going to be a happy ending. It could well be that what we will see with weak cucked populations is a great die off, followed by social chaos, as the system that allowed all of this BS to flourish collapses. It then will be like any other ecological community in nature, when food resources are no longer available. Welcome to the zombie apocalypse!

The Coming Nordicide

One of the issues not dealt with by the white nationalist is inter-racial survival, particularly the sub-racial groups such as Nordic, northern Europeans. In fact, some open-minded "nationalist" were quite willing to bash anyone concerned about this, and daring to write on that theme. (Might as well join the system than join those guys.) The Nordic racial group is under the strongest attack, part of it methodological, that is, being defined not to exist by the otherwise identity conscious elites, the same elites who see the entire universe as a social construction with a million types of gender, and then there is outright attack.

By "Nordics," I mean not merely Scandinavians, but the generally light haired, light eyed northern Europeans, such as the descendants of the Anglo Saxons. Madison Grant gave a classic account, and there are more recent racial theorists dealing with this, and I will report on it, if still breathing in the future.

https://www.amazon.com/Passing-Great-Race-Madison-Grant/dp/1471022935

Anyway, apart from movie caricatures and stereotypes, as either Nazis if male, or whores, if female, there is the day-to-day oppression:

https://summit.news/2020/09/17/teacher-tells-student-she-doesnt-have-the-right-to-an-opinion-because-shes-white-and-blonde/

A video clip shows a grandmother confronting a teacher over the phone about how she told a student she didn't have a right to an opinion because she was "white" and "blonde."

The footage starts with the grandmother explaining to the teacher that her granddaughter is crying and hasn't been to school because of this "BLM crap."

She then accuses the teacher of telling her granddaughter that she had no right to express an opinion on the issue because she's British, white and has blonde hair.

After being told there is an audio recording of the exchange, the teacher responds, "Well I can't remember, maybe."

The teacher then accuses the granddaughter Kelsey of having white privilege and saying she didn't "live through" what the other girl involved in the discussion (who was evidently black) had experienced.

It subsequently emerged that Kelsey had refused to honor Black Lives Matter and the teacher had immediately took the black student's side because "Kelsey isn't in a position to know how black girls feel.

Then there are these recent killings of Nordic Americans, for no other reason than the lightness of their skin, hair and eyes, triggering the killers. Interested readers can explore the shocking details:

https://www.unz.com/sbpdl/his-name-is-tyler-wingate-24-year-old-white-man-gets-in-car-accident-with-black-male-in-83-black-detroit-black-motorist-beats-him-to-death/

https://www.unz.com/sbpdl/his-name-is-cannon-hinnant-five-year-old-white-boy-shot-and-murdered-

execution-style-by-black-neighbor-for-riding-his-bike-
in-his-lawn/

No White Lives Matter riots here, only White pathology, or apathy about these deaths.

In future essays I intend to write more on Nordic survival with an eye to collecting it all as a book. [Yep, this is it, but more to come!] We have a right to exist, and I think, to have my racial sub-group eliminated basically drains the world of value for me. Why create a wonderful world of plenty, with the fantastic economic system, if it is in the end only for the Chinese and Africans, and our kind disappears? That is universalism gone mad. Resist!

www.ingramcontent.com/pod-product-compliance
Lightning Source LLC
Chambersburg PA
CBHW070755240726
48654CB00007B/87